Making Musical Apps

Peter Brinkmann

O'REILLY®

Beijing · Cambridge · Farnham · Köln · Sebastopol · Tokyo

Making Musical Apps
by Peter Brinkmann

Published by O'Reilly Media, Inc., 1005 Gravenstein Highway North, Sebastopol, CA 95472.

O'Reilly books may be purchased for educational, business, or sales promotional use. Online editions are also available for most titles (*http://my.safaribooksonline.com*). For more information, contact our corporate/institutional sales department: (800) 998-9938 or *corporate@oreilly.com*.

Editor: Shawn Wallace	**Cover Designer:** Karen Montgomery
Production Editor: Kristen Borg	**Interior Designer:** David Futato
Proofreader: O'Reilly Production Services	**Illustrator:** Robert Romano

Revision History for the First Edition:
    2012-02-15   First release
See *http://oreilly.com/catalog/errata.csp?isbn=9781449314903* for release details.

ISBN: 978-1-449-31490-3

[LSI]

1329319781

Table of Contents

Preface

Pure Data (Pd) is a programming language for digital audio and more. Written by Miller Puckette in the 1990s and under active development ever since, Pd has established itself as one of the leading open-source packages for computer music, and it remains largely interoperable with its commercial cousin, Max/MSP. A Pd program, called a *patch*, is a graphical representation of the flow of audio signals and control messages in a piece of music that Pd will execute in real time; changes to a patch take effect immediately. Its interactive and visual nature accounts for much of the appeal of Pd.

Pd has been popular in computer music circles since its appearance in 1996, and recent years have seen its adoption in commercial projects, most notably the computer game *Spore* by Electronic Arts and *Inception the App* by Reality Jockey Ltd., which made the *London Times* list of top 500 iPhone apps.

Inception the App is based on *libpd*, a thin layer on top of Pd that turns Pd into an embeddable audio library. Since the appearance of libpd in July 2010, a growing number of developers have been using libpd in their projects. Other noteworthy examples include *Sonaur* for Android, *NodeBeat* for Android and iOS, and *Pugs Luv Beats* for iOS.

This book is about libpd as an audio engine for mobile apps. We will focus on musical apps that require sophisticated audio processing capabilities, but libpd also has potential as an audio engine for games. As processors become more powerful, games may reduce their use of canned samples and synthesize music and sound effects instead. Procedural audio in games has much creative and expressive potential, and libpd is an excellent platform for it.

This book is primarily aimed at developers who want to equip their mobile apps with audio capabilities that go beyond the mere triggering of samples, as well as composers and sound designers who want to deploy their work on mobile devices. If you are managing a project with multiple developers, the discussion of the delineation of the interface between audio components and the rest of the app will help you structure roles and responsibilities in your team.

Conventions Used in This Book

The following typographical conventions are used in this book:

Italic

> Indicates new terms, URLs, email addresses, filenames, and file extensions.

`Constant width`

> Used for program listings, as well as within paragraphs to refer to program elements such as variable or function names, databases, data types, environment variables, statements, and keywords.

`Constant width bold`

> Shows commands or other text that should be typed literally by the user.

`Constant width italic`

> Shows text that should be replaced with user-supplied values or by values determined by context.

 This icon signifies a tip, suggestion, or general note.

 This icon indicates a warning or caution.

Using Code Examples

This book is here to help you get your job done. In general, you may use the code in this book in your programs and documentation. You do not need to contact us for permission unless you're reproducing a significant portion of the code. For example, writing a program that uses several chunks of code from this book does not require permission. Selling or distributing a CD-ROM of examples from O'Reilly books does require permission. Answering a question by citing this book and quoting example code does not require permission. Incorporating a significant amount of example code from this book into your product's documentation does require permission.

We appreciate, but do not require, attribution. An attribution usually includes the title, author, publisher, and ISBN. For example: "*Making Musical Apps* by Peter Brinkmann (O'Reilly). Copyright 2012 Peter Brinkmann, 978-1-4493-1490-3."

If you feel your use of code examples falls outside fair use or the permission given above, feel free to contact us at *permissions@oreilly.com*.

Safari® Books Online

Safari Books Online is an on-demand digital library that lets you easily search over 7,500 technology and creative reference books and videos to find the answers you need quickly.

With a subscription, you can read any page and watch any video from our library online. Read books on your cell phone and mobile devices. Access new titles before they are available for print, and get exclusive access to manuscripts in development and post feedback for the authors. Copy and paste code samples, organize your favorites, download chapters, bookmark key sections, create notes, print out pages, and benefit from tons of other time-saving features.

O'Reilly Media has uploaded this book to the Safari Books Online service. To have full digital access to this book and others on similar topics from O'Reilly and other publishers, sign up for free at *http://my.safaribooksonline.com*.

How to Contact Us

Please address comments and questions concerning this book to the publisher:

O'Reilly Media, Inc.
1005 Gravenstein Highway North
Sebastopol, CA 95472
800-998-9938 (in the United States or Canada)
707-829-0515 (international or local)
707-829-0104 (fax)

We have a web page for this book, where we list errata, examples, and any additional information. You can access this page at:

http://shop.oreilly.com/product/0636920022503.do

To comment or ask technical questions about this book, send email to:

bookquestions@oreilly.com

For more information about our books, courses, conferences, and news, see our website at *http://www.oreilly.com*.

Find us on Facebook: *http://facebook.com/oreilly*

Follow us on Twitter: *http://twitter.com/oreillymedia*

Watch us on YouTube: *http://www.youtube.com/oreillymedia*

Acknowledgments

The material discussed in this book grew out of the work of many people, most of whom have been volunteering their time and expertise. Miller Puckette created Pure Data and made it available as open source. Miller was also an early supporter of libpd. Without his willingness to consider libpd-related patches to Pd itself, libpd would not be able to track the development of Pd as closely as it does now.

Naim Falandino, Scott Fitzgerald, Peter Kirn, and Hans-Christoph Steiner developed a partial Android port of Pd that paved the way for libpd. Peter and Hans-Christoph remain deeply involved with the project, and libpd owes much of its success to their work.

Chris McCormick took an early version of libpd and ran with it, creating PdWebkit-Droid as well as PdDroidParty, two promising platforms for deploying content created with Pd. He also contributed to the build system and the Python branch.

Martin Roth and Dominik Hierner at Reality Jockey Ltd. created the first version of the iOS components of libpd, and Michael Breidenbrücker approved their release as open source. Joe White and Rob Thomas spent much time answering my questions about RjDj, as did Frank Barknecht, who also donated an RjDj scene for distribution with libpd.

Richard Lawler contributed the first sample projects for iOS and helped maintain the Objective-C bindings.

Dan Wilcox created a C++ wrapper for libpd and integrated it into openFrameworks.

Rich Eakin greatly improved the way libpd manages patch files. He also drove the recent revision of the iOS components, completely revamping the audio glue and updating it for iOS 5.

Shawn Wallace, my editor at O'Reilly, was the first to suggest that libpd deserves book-length treatment, and he saw the project through from proposal to publication. I am grateful for the opportunity to write this book, and for all his work throughout the process. It's been a great experience.

Thanks also to the technical reviewers, Shawn Greenlee and Chris McCormick, as well as my colleagues at Google, Ananya Misra and Andrew Senior, who performed the internal publication review.

This book ties together several areas that have long been interests of mine, including music, software, and electronics. I wouldn't have picked up those skills if my parents hadn't encouraged and supported all my pursuits from an early age. I am grateful to them.

Finally, thanks to my wonderful wife, Shiau-uen, who has remained remarkably tolerant of the long (as well as odd) hours that have gone into the development of libpd and the writing of this book.

CHAPTER 1

Introduction

Pure Data is a great audio engine; it is powerful, flexible, and extensible. With the appearance of libpd, its range has grown beyond the desktop to mobile and embedded settings. Its permissive BSD license allows developers to add libpd to virtually any project. The complete absence of dependencies means that you can build libpd as soon as you have a C compiler. Ready-made bindings for Java and Objective-C as well as support for Android and iOS help you get mobile apps off the ground in a hurry.

One of the most attractive features of Pd is its instantaneous interactive nature; you change the signal processing graph on the screen while Pd is running, and you hear the effect immediately. This makes it an excellent tool for prototyping audio components, especially for games.

In the past, game developers have rigged up development setups that connect a game to Pd using the networking capabilities of Pd. While this is an effective way of creating preliminary audio components, a prototype created in this way will always be a prototype, and the use of network objects in Pd introduces some friction into the patching process. In order to deploy components created in this manner, developers have to reimplement them in a format that can be shipped with the game.

With libpd, all these inefficiencies disappear. Sound designers can prototype audio components in Pd, using the same objects and techniques that they would use when creating a patch for any other purpose. When the patch is done, the app developer simply adds it to the resources of the app, much like a media file. The UI elements that the designer uses when creating and testing a patch become the conduit through which the app controls the patch.

The design of libpd achieves complete separation of concerns between audio development and app development, as well as a smooth workflow from prototyping to production. *With libpd, the prototype is the production code.*

A Great Investment

Learning Pure Data in general and libpd in particular is a great investment. In a technological environment that changes so quickly that many books are out of date before they are published, Pure Data is a rare pocket of stability. Realizing that many works in computer music are at risk of being lost because they depend on obsolete technology, Miller Puckette designed Pd to be a durable and stable platform, and he started the Pd Repertory project, which aims to port valuable compositions to Pd in order to preserve them for posterity.

In a similar vein, libpd aims to provide a stable API for embedded audio that behaves in much the same way across a wide variety of platforms and languages and protects the developer from the ever-changing arcana of current technology, providing a level of abstraction that lets you focus on the work at hand. Think of it as your insanity abstraction layer. That doesn't mean that libpd won't change; both Pd and libpd are under active development, but most changes will happen under the hood, without affecting the API that client code depends on.

At the Pure Data Convention 2011 in Weimar, I participated in a panel discussion on the future of Pd. There was no shortage of ideas for improvements; a better user interface, faster release cycle, optimizations for modern processors, etc. What really struck me, however, was that nobody suggested new audio processing capabilities. Fifteen years after the appearance of Pd, people have yet to reach the limits of Pd as a synthesis engine. The mathematics at the core of Pd is as powerful now as it was in 1996, and Miller's understanding of it is second to none. That's the real reason why Pd is here to stay.

Resources

The main project repository of libpd is available at GitHub. In addition to the core library and components for Android and iOS, you can find support for other languages as well as some loosely associated projects. If you're handy with a soldering iron and not afraid to try experimental hardware, you can find instructions for building and using a Bluetooth-MIDI interface for Android devices. You can also find much documentation in the project wiki at GitHub.

The libpd community meets at Pd Everywhere; you can find a link at *http://shop.oreilly.com/product/0636920022503.do*. In less than a year, Pd Everywhere has grown from a fledgling site to an active group of more than 200 developers, ranging from core maintainers to casual users. The tone is always helpful and civil, with an amazing signal-to-noise ratio. If you run into a problem with libpd, you should turn to Pd Everywhere first. We'll be happy to hear from you. Finally, if you have a question about Pd itself rather than the libpd wrapper, you can turn to the Pd mailing list.

Prerequisites

This book assumes that you have some working knowledge of Android or iOS programming, as well as a working development environment. If you're just getting started, I recommend *Learning Android* by Marko Gargenta (O'Reilly) as well as *Professional Android 2 Application Development* by Reto Meier (Wrox) for Android; and *Programming iOS 5* by Matt Neuburg (O'Reilly) as well as *Learning iOS Programming* by Alasdair Allan (O'Reilly) for iOS.

You will need to be able to run sample applications on an actual device instead of just emulating or simulating one in software. Only testing an app with the Android emulator or iPhone simulator is not enough. This is a common admonition, but in the case of musical apps it applies twofold. Generally speaking, you need to test your apps on an actual device because an app that works just fine in simulation may fail in the wild. When doing audio, however, you also have the converse problem — an app that produces glitchy audio in simulation may work just fine when running on a real device. One way or another, testing in simulation will tell you little about the quality of an app.

Android Setup

The Android team recommends Eclipse for Android development, and so that's what we'll be using. You'll need a recent version of the Android Software Development Kit (SDK), a recent version of Eclipse, and the Android Development Tools (ADT) for Eclipse. The Android developer site explains how to set all this up (*http://developer.android.com/sdk/installing.html*). Make sure to use Eclipse 3.7 or later; older versions will give you much grief. Even though libpd itself is written in C, you won't need to install the Android Native Development Toolkit (NDK) if you just want to write libpd-based apps in Java.

The Android development environment can be tricky to set up. Follow the steps very carefully and try a few of the sample apps that come with the SDK to convince yourself that your installation is ready for Android development.

 A complete Android development environment consists of several separate but interconnected pieces: Eclipse, Java Development Kit (JDK), ADT, SDK, and NDK. This is an occasional cause of confusion because they are all updated independently; you need to choose versions that will work together. As a general rule, the maintainers of libpd aim to make things work with the latest version of all components, but sometimes it may take a while to catch up. When in doubt, check the libpd wiki for the currently recommended setup.

The installation tool of the Android SDK will ask you which SDK versions to download. I recommend that you select all of them and install new ones as they become available, even if you only intend to target older versions. You can deploy libpd-based apps to API Level 3 (Cupcake) or higher, but you will need at least API Level 10 to build an app with libpd.

In addition to Android SDK versions, you need to pay attention to Java compiler settings. Pd for Android requires Java 1.6. Each project in Pd for Android explicitly enforces this requirement, but you should still select Preferences → Java → Compiler and make sure that the compiler compliance level of your workspace is set to 1.6 and that Java 1.6 is installed on your machine. If this conflicts with other projects of yours, I recommend that you create a new workspace for projects that use libpd.

 In the past, different versions of the ADT have taken different approaches to laying out and configuring projects. The Android branch of libpd tracks the development of the ADT, and we make an effort to remain compatible with the latest version. This means that you will need Version 15 or later of the ADT, regardless of which version of Android you are developing for.

If a future upgrade of the ADT breaks a project of yours, you can update your project configuration by opening its context menu and selecting Android Tools → Fix Project Properties.

The Android emulator is extremely limited in its audio capabilities. At the time of writing, it will only do audio at a sample rate of 8000Hz, and the round-trip audio latency from microphone to speaker is quite large. You will need to run your app on an actual device if you want to test its audio performance.

iOS Setup

Setting up a Mac for iOS development is straightforward; if you install Xcode 4.2, you'll automatically get all the components you need, including the revision control system Git. Xcode 4.2 is quite different from earlier versions, and you should consider upgrading if you haven't done so already.

In particular, Xcode 4.2 introduced *Automatic Reference Counting (ARC)*. The iOS branch of libpd is built without ARC, but this choice does not affect client code. Projects using libpd will work equally well regardless of whether ARC is enabled. Since Apple recommends ARC for new development, the sample projects in this book will use it, but we will also point out the minor differences to keep in mind when building projects without ARC.

You will need an iOS device for testing, and you need to be able to run your own apps on it. That requires enrolling in Apple's iOS Developer Program and paying a fee. The simulator tends to produce glitchy audio, and it doesn't support all audio session categories and channel configurations. The maintainers of the iOS branch of libpd are making every effort to allow for at least some basic testing in simulation, but the simulator has been a moving target so far. Give it a try, but don't expect it to work in all situations.

Git

Git is a relatively new revision control system that's becoming more and more popular. You will need it for downloading and updating all libraries discussed in this book. Knowledge of Git is not a prerequisite, and we will list all Git commands that you will need to work with libpd. If you intend to manage your libpd-based projects with Git (and I highly recommend that you do), then you need to study up on Git. Many excellent tutorials are available online.

Coming from the Linux world, Git is most at home in a terminal. There are a few graphical frontends for Git, but none of them seem entirely convincing at this time. If you're using Linux or Mac OS X, you can use the built-in terminal. If you're using Windows, use the GitBash tool that comes with the distribution of Git. If you're unfamiliar with the Unix command line, you should study up on basic shell commands. It won't take long, and it's a useful skill to have.

The way to install Git depends on your operating system. If you're using a Mac, Git will be included in the installation of Xcode 4.2. If you're using one of the popular Linux distributions, search for Git in your package manager and install the basic Git package. Windows users can find installation archives online. The most basic one will do—just make sure to select GitBash when prompted.

 If you're doing Android development, you may be aware of EGit, a Git plugin for Eclipse. EGit is not adequate for our purposes because libpd and its branches are organized in terms of Git submodules and EGit doesn't support submodules yet.

On the iOS side, Xcode 4.2 has some Git support baked right into it, but that won't cut it, either, for the same reason: poor handling of submodules.

CHAPTER 2

Making Noise with Pure Data

This chapter gives a brief overview of Pure Data, focusing on the most important features from the point of view of libpd. If you're already familiar with Pd, you will learn how to create patches that work well with libpd. If you aren't yet familiar with Pd, you will learn how to create simple patches that will go beep on demand, just enough to create mocks for testing while you're waiting for your sound designer to come through.

This chapter is not a thorough introduction to Pd—nor does it need to be, because excellent books on Pd have already been written. I highly recommend *Theory and Technique of Electronic Music* by Miller Puckette (World Scientific), as well as *Designing Sound* by Andy Farnell (MIT Press), which includes a tutorial introduction to Pd that's available online as a free excerpt. Both books cover Pd as well as a wide range of other fascinating topics, but they are not for the casual reader. If you are looking for a gentle introduction to Pd, the free *FLOSS Manual (http://flossmanuals.net/puredata/)* as well as Johannes Kreidler's *Pd Tutorial* (Wolke Verlag, *http://www.pd-tutorial.com/*) will serve you well.

Installing Pure Data

You can download Pure Data from *http://puredata.info/*. You will find two flavors of Pd there, Pd Vanilla and Pd Extended. Make sure to choose Pd Vanilla because that's the branch that libpd tracks. You generally want to choose the latest stable release.

If you're new to the world of open source software, you may be concerned about low version numbers like 0.43. Don't worry, though. Open source developers tend to be extremely conservative in their assignment of version numbers, and serious open source projects are polished and rock solid long before they hit Version 1.0.

After you launch Pd, you will see a window like the one in Figure 2-1. This is Pd-0.43-0 on a Mac. If you are using a different operating system or version of Pd, your window may look different, but the salient features for now are the same: You should see a large empty text field, as well as a checkbox labeled DSP (for digital signal processing) or Compute Audio in the upper righthand corner. When working with Pd, it's a good idea to keep an eye on the text field because that's where Pd will print status updates and error messages. The checkbox indicates whether the signal processing components of Pd are active. When you launch Pd, make sure to switch DSP on. If you expect to get a sound from Pd but don't hear anything, look at the DSP checkbox first.

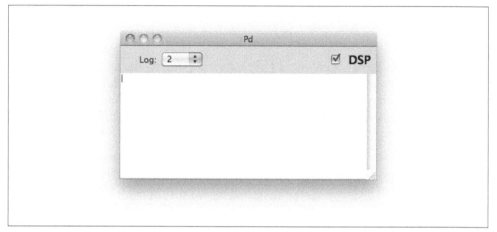

Figure 2-1. Main window of Pd-0.43-0 on a Mac

 If you're already familiar with Pd, you may be used to controlling the DSP toggle from within your patch, with messages like `pd dsp 1`. Such messages will still work in libpd, but they are usually redundant because libpd provides other ways to enable or disable signal processing. (See Chapter 5 and Chapter 6 for details.) I recommend that you leave the DSP toggle alone when patching for libpd.

Let's make sure that Pd is working properly: Select the menu item "Media → Test Audio and MIDI...". You will see a window that looks like Figure 2-2.

Select 60dB or 80dB under TEST TONES. If you hear a sine tone, you can close the test window; your installation of Pd is ready. If you don't hear anything even though your test tone and DSP toggle are on, then the trouble shooting begins — are your speakers plugged in and switched on, did you mute the audio, is some other program hogging the audio interface, etc. A well-crafted Google search will usually turn up a solution, and if all else fails, you can turn to the Pd mailing list for help.

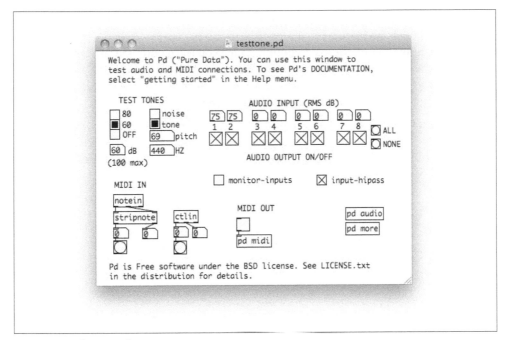

Figure 2-2. Pd test window

A First Patch

Let's create our first Pd patch. Select File → New. (For clarity, I'll spell out the menu items here, but nobody actually uses menus when patching. Using keyboard shortcuts for the most important operations quickly becomes second nature.) You'll see an empty canvas (Figure 2-3).

Figure 2-3. The beauty of a blank canvas

This looks quite different from other graphical user interfaces. It offers no guidance, no buttons to click, no features to discover. A usability expert would decry the tyranny of the blank canvas. Don't despair, though. Once you learn your way around Pd, you'll appreciate the clarity that comes with the absence of visual clutter. Pd makes no assumptions as to what you want to do, or how you want to do it. A blank canvas may seem daunting, but it is the right foundation for creative work.

Select the menu item Put → Object. You'll see a dashed box that will follow your mouse pointer. Move it to the center of your canvas and type **osc~ 220** into the box. Now click outside the box and the box will become solid. You have just created a sinusoid with a frequency of 220Hz (Figure 2-4).

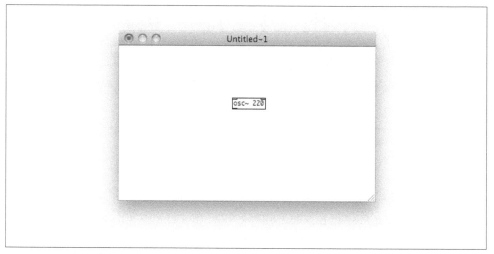

Figure 2-4. First Pd object

You won't hear anything yet, but that's okay for now. Select Put → Object again, place the dashed box under your oscillator, type in ***~ 0.1**, and click outside the box. You have created a multiplier object (Figure 2-5).

Create another object, place it under your multiplier, and type in **dac~**. That's a digital-to-analog converter, and it represents your audio interface (Figure 2-6). You still won't hear anything because our objects aren't connected yet. Each object is already working; in particular, the oscillator is already generating a sine tone, but the sine tone isn't going anywhere. We'll change that now.

You have probably noticed the little boxes, empty or solid, that Pd draws in the corners of your objects. They are the inlets and outlets through which your objects communicate with one another. The general picture is that data flows from top to bottom; inlets are at the top of your objects, outlets are at the bottom.

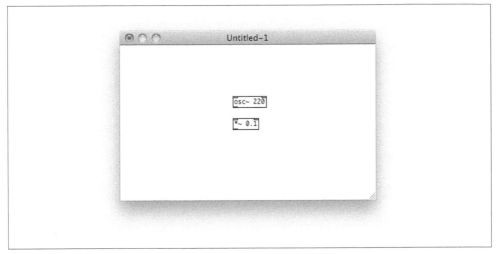

Figure 2-5. Second Pd object

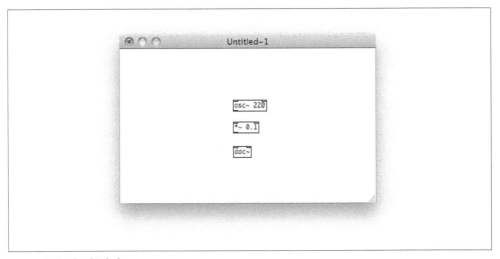

Figure 2-6. Third Pd object

Now we connect the objects by dragging outlets to inlets. Specifically, move your mouse pointer to the lower lefthand corner of your oscillator object. When you're on top of the outlet, the mouse pointer will look like a circle. Now drag your mouse to the left inlet of your multiplier. You don't have to be terribly precise; as long as your mouse pointer is inside the multiplier box and in the general vicinity of the left inlet, Pd will make the correct connection when you release the mouse button (Figure 2-7).

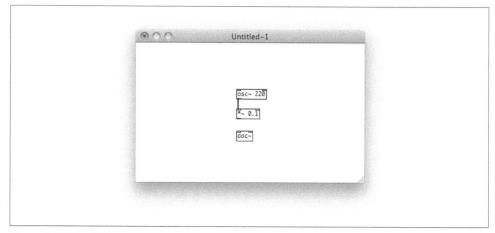

Figure 2-7. First Pd connection

 Chances are that you have encountered the autoconnect feature of Pd by now: If you add a new object while an existing object is selected, Pd will automatically connect the first outlet of the selected object to the first inlet of the new object. This feature is quite convenient if you want to assemble a chain of objects in a hurry, but it can be surprising if you trigger it by accident. You can avoid confusion by always clicking on a blank spot of your canvas before adding a new object.

You still won't hear anything because the inlets of the audio interface are still unconnected. Now, if you connect the outlet of the multiplier to the left inlet of the audio interface, you will hear a tone in your left stereo channel. You can also draw a second connection from the outlet to the right channel, for a more balanced listening experience (Figure 2-8).

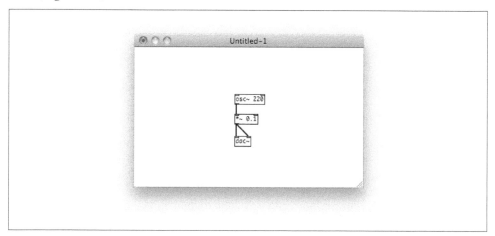

Figure 2-8. Second Pd connection

We've built our first signal processing chain: An oscillator creates samples, a multiplier reduces the amplitude for the protection of your ears, and the result is sent to the audio interface.

 When working with libpd, make sure that your output samples will always be between -1 and 1. Depending on your setting, out-of-range samples may cause a number of artifacts, ranging from mild distortion to plain noise. libpd will *not* clip your output for you. This was a deliberate design decision; automatic clipping would be convenient initially, but it wouldn't solve any problems, only sweep them under the rug. Ultimately, each patch is responsible for its output.

DC bias is a related concern; if it is at all possible that your patch may generate biased output (i.e., a signal whose mean value over time differs from zero), then you should consider adding a high-pass filter that will remove any constant components from your signal. Figure 2-9 shows a common pattern that eliminates DC bias as well as out-of-range samples by splicing hip~ and clip~ objects into each output channel.

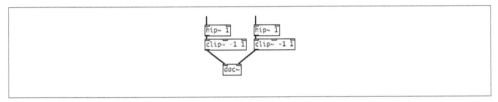

Figure 2-9. Eliminating DC bias and out-of-range samples

You should spend some time experimenting with the user interface. You can drag objects around and edit their properties by clicking inside them and typing in new values. You may want to try different frequencies and multipliers (keep your multipliers small, for the sake of your eardrums). Deleting connections is straightforward, just select a connection and hit backspace. Deleting objects is a little trickier: Drag your mouse to select a region containing the objects that you want to delete, then hit backspace.

Notice that you can modify your patch in real time. When you change the frequency of your oscillator, you hear the change immediately. When you delete a connection, the corresponding signal disappears immediately. There is no need to compile your edits; any change becomes effective the moment you make it. This is one of the reasons why Pd is such a nimble prototyping tool.

Pd has two modes, edit mode and run mode. For the time being, our activities take place in edit mode. If you open a new canvas or add an object, Pd will automatically go into edit mode, and so you won't immediately have to worry about what mode you're in. If, however, you find that Pd mysteriously refuses to let you edit a patch, take a look at your mouse pointer. In edit mode, it will look like a hand; in run mode, like an arrow. If you are in the wrong mode, just toggle the menu item Edit → Edit Mode.

Now is a good time to familiarize yourself with the help feature of Pd: Right-click on an object and select Help. You'll see a patch that illustrates and explains this object. If you right-click and select Help in an empty area of your canvas, you'll get to a help patch that lists all built-in objects of Pd. You can learn a lot about Pd by just going through this list and looking at the help patches of various objects.

Adding Audio Input

We will now add audio input to our patch. You probably want to use headphones to avoid feedback.

Return to the patch we created in the previous step and delete the connection from the oscillator to the multiplier. Now add an object and type in **adc~**. Add another object and type in ***~**. The former is an analog-to-digital converter, i.e., audio input. The latter is another multiplier, but unlike our first multiplier it will multiply two audio signals together rather than multiply one signal by a constant.

Connect the outlets of the audio input to the left inlet of the new multiplier. (If an inlet is connected to several outlets, the signals are added implicitly.) Connect the outlet of the oscillator to the other inlet of the new multiplier, and connect the outlet of the new multiplier to the left inlet of the original multiplier (Figure 2-10).

If you speak into your microphone, the patch will add a metallic twang to your voice. This effect is known as a ring modulator, and it is an easy way to create robotic voices, used to great effect by the Daleks from *Doctor Who*. Now is a good time to save your patch as, say, *ringmod.pd*.

Sample Rates and Audio Channels

The most important parameters for the configuration of libpd are the sample rate and the number of input/output channels. When patching for Pd on the desktop, you are usually free to choose any sample rate you like. Moreover, CPU cycles and power consumption are not much of a concern, and so the desired sound quality is the main factor that determines the sample rate.

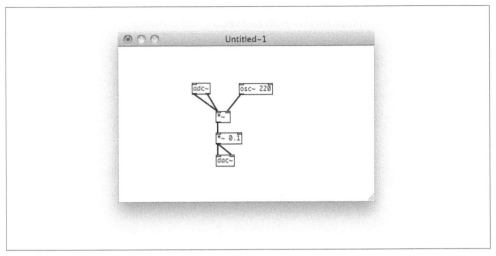

Figure 2-10. Ring modulator

On a resource-constrained mobile device, however, the situation is quite different. The set of supported sample rates may be quite limited. In addition to sound quality, you will have to consider CPU power and battery life when choosing your sample rate. Moreover, even if you determine that you can afford to operate at a high sample rate, you should check whether you actually have anything to gain from it. If you are going to process samples from the built-in microphone, for example, the input may be of such low quality that it makes little sense to choose a high sample rate in your app.

If at all possible, create patches that will work for a wide range of sample rates. If you are using samples, try to include versions for various common sample rates, such as 22050Hz and 44100Hz, and design your patch so that it checks the sample rate and selects the appropriate samples at runtime. libpd does not limit the number of channels, but on most mobile devices you won't get more than stereo.

 Pd will let you change the global sample rate with a little-known, un-documented message. Don't do this when patching for libpd — your client code will not notice the change and mayhem will ensue. There is, however, a well-documented way to change the local sample rate in subpatches, e.g., for synthesis techniques that require oversampling. (Look up the documentation of the block~ object if you'd like to learn more about this.) This is perfectly fine for libpd because it's all internal to Pd and won't affect the way libpd communicates with the outside world.

Control Rate Objects and Messages

So far we have only seen objects that work with audio signals. Such objects are on all the time and handle streams of audio samples. They are fundamental to signal processing, but they do not allow us to express events in time, such as a performer pressing a key on a piano or a game triggering sound effects. For expressing events, Pd provides another class of objects that are idle most of the time and only spring into action when needed.

Go back to *ringmod.pd* and select Put → Number. Place the new object above your oscillator and connect its outlet to the left inlet of the oscillator (Figure 2-11).

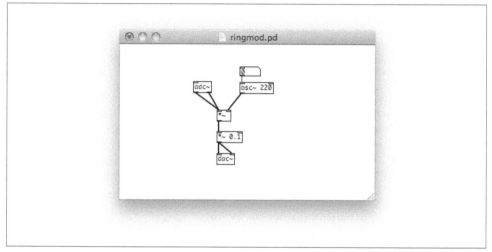

Figure 2-11. Adjustable ring modulator

So far, there has been no audible effect; the number object hasn't done anything yet, and your oscillator still oscillates at 220Hz. We will change that now. First, toggle Edit → Edit Mode to enter run mode. You can now change the frequency of your oscillator by dragging the value of the number box up or down, or you can click inside the number box, type in the value you want and hit Return. If you choose a value of 30, for instance, you will get the vocal effect as used in the original Daleks episode from *Doctor Who*.

Behind the scenes, every time you enter a value, the number object will send a *number message* containing the new value to the oscillator, and the oscillator will make the incoming number its new frequency. When you aren't interacting with the number box, it will just sit idle. When your number box receives a number message in its inlet, it will update itself and send the new value to its outlet.

If you play with the new object for a little while, you'll notice that it is a bit awkward to use because it takes large mouse movements to get to frequencies above, say, 1000Hz. Switch back to edit mode, add a new object above your number object, type in **mtof**, and connect its outlet to the inlet of the number object. The `mtof` object takes MIDI note values and maps them to frequencies, e.g., the MIDI note value 69 (middle A) maps to a frequency of 440Hz. Then add another number object on top of that and connect its outlet to the inlet of the `mtof` object (Figure 2-12).

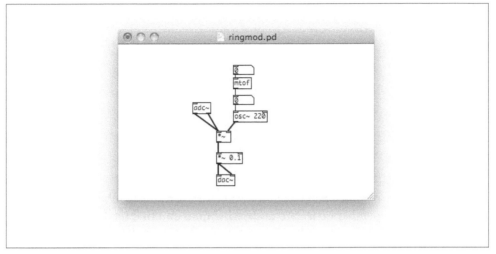

Figure 2-12. Improved adjustable ring modulator

 Don't be confused by the fact that we're using MIDI note values without using a MIDI controller; some of the MIDI functionality of Pd is useful even when you aren't using any MIDI devices.

If you switch to run mode and enter a value of, say, **69** in the top number box, you'll see a value of **440** in your original number box. Now you can easily sweep through the full range of human hearing with a single mouse gesture.

Note that messages only travel one way; the MIDI note box will affect the frequency box, but changes to the frequency box will not propagate back to the MIDI note box.

Sending and Receiving Messages

So far all our messages have been transmitted by wires, but that's not the only way. Pd also supports wireless messaging via send and receive objects. In order to see how this works, add a new object on top of your latest number object, type in **r midinote**, and connect the outlet of the new object to the inlet of the number object below. Add yet another number object, off to the right, and add a new object box below. Type **s midinote** into the object box and connect its inlet to the outlet of the new number object (Figure 2-13).

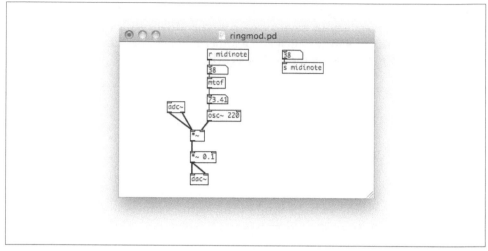

Figure 2-13. Wireless messaging with send and receive

If you switch to run mode and change the value of your new number box, you'll see that the other two number boxes are updated with it, and that the frequency of your oscillator also changes accordingly. Behind the scenes, the send object takes messages from its inlet and passes them on to all receiver objects for the same symbol.

> When using libpd, most of the communication between Pd and the outside world happens via send and receive symbols. In addition to the sample rate and number of channels, the set of send and receive symbols is another crucial component of the setup of libpd.

The send symbol in our example is a global symbol, i.e., if you create another canvas and add a receiver for this symbol, the new receiver will also respond to messages sent from your original canvas. If you want to limit your transmissions to your current patch, you can use the $0 tag, which Pd will expand into a number that uniquely identifies the patch that contains it. A common pattern is to prepend $0, e.g., `$0-midinote`.

The libpd API provides access to the $0 tag of the top-level patch of a Pd file, and so your app can address individual patches that it opened directly. If a file references other patches, known as *abstractions* in this context, then Pd will load and use them as expected, but libpd will remain unaware of them.

As a general matter of design, I recommend that you build your patches so that your app treats patches as black boxes, without having to know about abstractions and other implementation details; your code will be much more robust and maintainable that way. If you really can't avoid entangling your app with your abstractions, then you can rig up a communication scheme that lets your abstractions register themselves with your app upon loading.

Using send and receive objects is the most explicit way of sending messages without wires. You can also set up your number objects for wireless communication. In order to see how this works, delete the send object underneath your new number box. Right-click on the number box and select Properties (Figure 2-14).

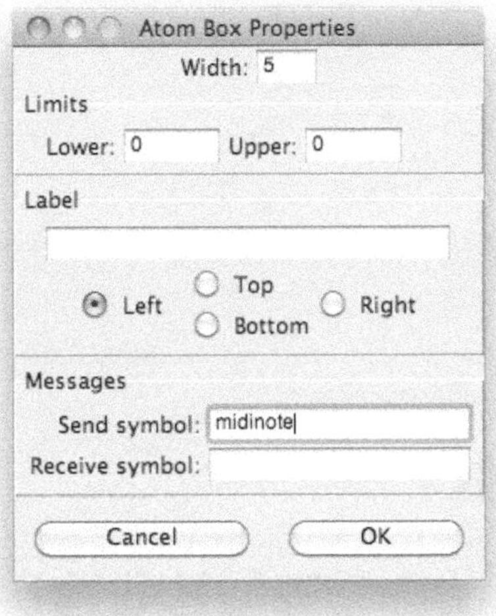

Figure 2-14. Pd properties dialog

Enter **midinote** next to "Send symbol" in the properties dialog and click on OK. Now, if you change the value of the number box, the new values are still distributed to the rest of the patch. This works nicely, but the patch is now harder to understand because it is not obvious that this number box has a send symbol. In order to remedy this, open the properties dialog again and enter an expressive label, e.g., **s:midinote**.

Similarly, delete the receive object, open the properties dialog of the number box underneath, enter **midinote** next to "Receive symbol" and choose a label, e.g., **r:midi note** (Figure 2-15). Convince yourself that the wireless communication between number boxes still works as before.

When patching for libpd, sound designers can use familiar GUI widgets in Pd. In order to prepare a patch for deployment to a libpd-based app, all they need to do is assign the agreed-upon send and receive symbols to these widgets. When the patch is deployed, the same GUI widgets that the sound designer used for testing become the conduit through which libpd controls the patch. The workflow is virtually frictionless; this is how libpd erases the distinction between prototype and production code.

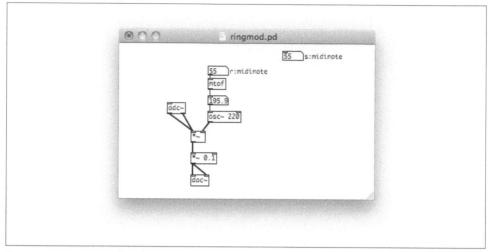

Figure 2-15. Using send and receive symbols

More About Messages

Let's make a rudimentary synthesizer. Go back to your previous patch and save it as *simple_synth.pd*. Now edit the adc~ object and type in **vline~** instead. Select Put → Message, place the resulting message box above your vline~ object, type in **0 2000**, and connect its outlet to the left inlet of the vline~ object. Repeat these steps but type in **1 1000** instead (Figure 2-16).

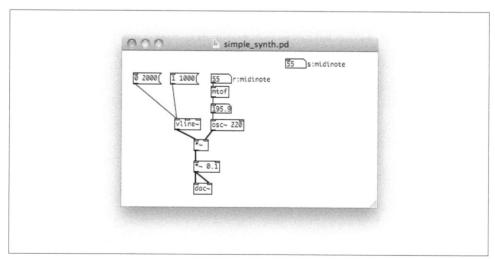

Figure 2-16. Envelope generator

The two message objects hold a new kind of message, a *list message*. If you switch to run mode and click on the second message (1 1000), you'll hear a sine tone ramping up from silence to full volume over the course of one second. If you click on the other message, you'll hear the sine tone ramping down to zero over the course of two seconds. The vline~ object provides transitions; the messages encode a target value (0 or 1 in our example) as well as the time in milliseconds that it takes to reach the new value.

The vline~ object understands other messages as well. Add another message box, wire it up like the other two, and type in **stop**. This message, a *symbol message*, will stop vline~ at its current value. In run mode, try clicking on the new message immediately after clicking on one of the other messages. You'll find that the transition stops.

Finally, let's create a sound with a multipart envelope. Add a new message box, wire it up like the others, and type in **1 10, 0 500 10** (Figure 2-17).

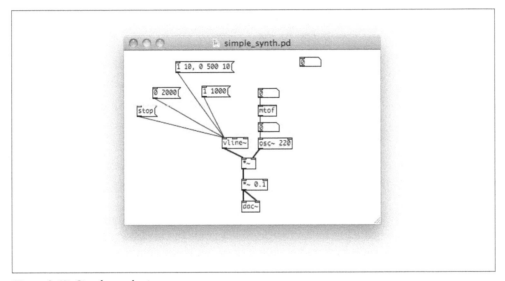

Figure 2-17. Simple synthesizer

This new box will send multiple messages to the vline~ object. The first message is familiar, just ramping up to 1 in 10ms. The second one is slightly more complicated. It tells vline~ to wait 10ms and then ramp down to 0 in 500ms. If you trigger this message, you'll hear a sharp attack, followed by a longer decay. Think of it as a first approximation of the envelope of a piano. You can still control the pitch with the number objects we added earlier.

In order to trigger such a message from libpd, you can use a bang message. Simply select Put → Bang and connect the outlet of the bang object to the inlet of your latest message box (Figure 2-18).

A bang is an empty message; it is ubiquitous in Pd patches and serves as a universal trigger. If you open the properties dialog of the bang object, you can equip it with send and receive symbols for easy integration with libpd.

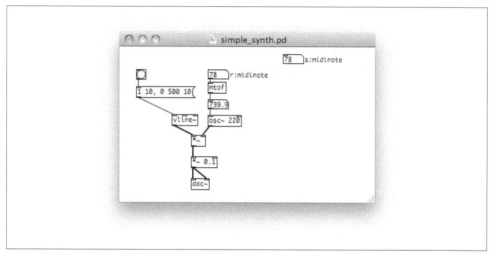

Figure 2-18. Triggering with a bang

Finally, we modify our patch to create a crude percussive instrument. Save the patch as *simple_percussion.pd*, edit the oscillator object, and type in **noise~**. Now, if you click on the bang object, you'll hear a short burst of noise. If you play with the durations in the envelope, you can make it sound more like a first approximation of a hi-hat.

The machinery for setting the pitch is still attached, but it no longer serves any purpose because **noise~** does not have a pitch. After deleting the obsolete parts, you'll have the beginnings of a percussive instrument (Figure 2-19).

The message types we have seen so far are bang, number, symbol, and list. In addition to these types, libpd also supports *typed messages*, which are important for controlling certain complex objects. We will see some examples in Chapter 3.

If you are familiar with data structures in Pd, then you have probably come across pointer messages. Pointer messages are the only message type that libpd doesn't support, because Pd pointers have no meaning outside of Pd. If you need to send pointer messages from libpd, you can store them in a pointer object in your patch and trigger them with a bang from libpd.

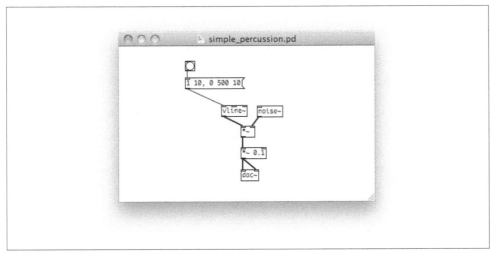

Figure 2-19. Basic percussion

Using MIDI with Pd

MIDI is a great way to connect disparate pieces of hardware. You can buy a USB-MIDI interface in 2012 and connect it to a synthesizer from 1983 and they will understand each other, no configuration required. Few other digital standards have lasted as long. Unfortunately, this strength becomes a liability when MIDI is used as a way of representing musical information in software, because it shoehorns musical expression into the limitations of a 30-year-old hardware protocol. Besides, MIDI support in an app based on libpd is usually redundant because MIDI events won't encode any information that regular Pd messages can't express.

If you want your patch to communicate with the world beyond your app, you should consider *Open Sound Control (OSC)* instead of MIDI. While Pd Vanilla does not support OSC out of the box, there are extensions of Pd, known as externals, that will add OSC capabilities to Pd, and you can use them in libpd-based apps. Since OSC only uses basic networking capabilities, it is a simple yet flexible way to allow your patch to communicate with the rest of the world.

Still, in some cases it may make sense to use MIDI in a musical app. Specifically, when creating a patch, it can be convenient to trigger sounds with a MIDI controller. In order to maintain a smooth workflow from patching to deployment, it may make sense to write the application code so that it controls the patch through the same MIDI objects that the sound designer used when creating the patch. The application code can control a patch through MIDI objects even if no MIDI controller is attached to the device. It's just a matter of calling the appropriate functions in libpd; Pd doesn't know or care whether those calls originate in hardware or in software.

For example, we can easily transform our simple synth into a MIDI synth by adding a few objects (Figure 2-20). The object `notein 1` receives note events on MIDI Channel 1, consisting of a pitch and a velocity. The pitch is a MIDI note value that we map to the frequency of our oscillator. The velocity is a value between 0 and 127 that we normalize to the range from zero to one, and we use it to control the peak amplitude of the vline~ object. The first entry, $1, of the message object `$1 10, 0 500 10` is a placeholder, and it will be replaced by the normalized velocity when a MIDI note event comes in.

If you want to try this patch with a MIDI device, you need to select "Preferences → MIDI Settings..." and choose the device that you want. If you don't have a physical MIDI controller, you can download and install a virtual MIDI keyboard. The built-in test patch of Pd that we used earlier in this chapter will also let you check your MIDI connections.

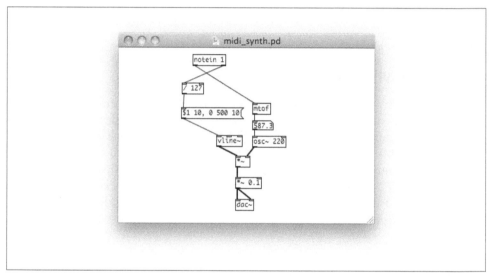

Figure 2-20. Basic MIDI synth

Note off events are mapped to note on events with velocity zero; if you hit a note on the keyboard and release it immediately, you'll notice that the note generated by Pd will be silenced right away. That's because releasing the key will result in the message `0 10, 0 500 10` being sent to vline~. The first part, 0 10, will ramp the output down to zero in ten milliseconds, and then the second part will be redundant. If you hit a key and hold it, the tone will fade away over the course of half a second, like before.

The Pd object for receiving MIDI pitch bend events, `bendin`, outputs pitch bend values ranging from 0 to 16383. The object for sending pitch bend events, `bendout`, expects input values ranging from -8192 to 8191. This discrepancy is a bug in Pd that probably won't be fixed in order not to break existing patches. If you find it necessary to use `bendin`, you should always subtract 8192 from its output.

Both Pd and libpd support input and output of the full range of standard MIDI events, but having a Pd patch output MIDI events only makes sense if the patch is supposed to control external MIDI hardware, such as a synthesizer. That is a rare use case for mobile apps.

Further Topics

Arrays play an important role in Pd. They are useful for storing samples or precomputed function values, and the user interface of Pd lets you view and modify arrays in real time. A complete discussion of the objects and techniques needed for patching with arrays is beyond the scope of this book, though; we just note that libpd gives read and write access to arrays in Pd. In addition to sample rate, channel counts, and send and receive symbols, the names of arrays to read from or write to are the last component of a complete specification of the interaction between Pd and a libpd-based app.

 Pd patches routinely resize their arrays, and libpd is equipped to handle changing array sizes. Still, code that properly handles changing arrays is considerably more complex than code for arrays of fixed size. If arrays are part of your interaction with libpd, I recommend that you choose a size at the beginning and then keep it fixed.

We have reached the end of our crash course, but we have still barely scratched the surface of Pure Data. We haven't discussed synthesis techniques, nor have we talked about flow control. As far as program flow is concerned, all our patches have been straight-line programs, taking messages from their origin to their destination without branching or looping. Pd is, however, a Turing-complete programming language, and it comes with powerful constructs for expressing the logic of a program, such as triggers, routing, and hot and cold inlets. All these are essential for serious work with Pd, and the references listed at the beginning of this chapter explain them nicely.

If you're looking to get started in a hurry, take a peek at rjlib, a collection of free, reusable components created by Reality Jockey Ltd. On the surface, its purpose is to help artists create scenes for Reality Jockey's RjDj app, but few of its components are specific to RjDj. In particular, you'll find a large collection of synthesizers, effects, and controllers that are ready to be used anywhere. We'll discuss rjlib in Chapter 3.

When Not to Make Musical Apps

What's easier than making a musical app with libpd? Why, using an existing app, of course! If your main goal is to run a Pd patch on a mobile device, then somebody else may already have done the heavy lifting for you.

RjDj by Reality Jockey Ltd. is the original Pd-based musical app, and it is much more than just a way to deploy Pd patches on iOS devices. The vision behind RjDj is that in the future, music on the go will no longer be limited to static mp3 files. Rather, music will come in the form of algorithmic compositions, known as *scenes*, that react to your activity level, lights and noise in your environment, and more. It will be the soundtrack to your life.

In this chapter, we'll be concerned with the more prosaic aspect of RjDj as a platform for deploying Pd patches. In a nutshell, if you want to create a musical app that reacts to sound, touch, and movement but doesn't require a sophisticated user interface, then RjDj may be a good choice. RjDj also provides basic support for displaying images and text. Another advantage of RjDj is that there's an Android version, ScenePlayer, that is mostly compatible with RjDj except for some recently added features. As long as your scene doesn't require sensor input beyond touch screen and accelerometer, it will work with both RjDj and ScenePlayer without requiring any changes. Chances are that ScenePlayer will support other sensors in the future, such as gyroscopes or GPS. RjDj and ScenePlayer are available as free downloads from the App Store and the Android Market, respectively.

If you need a sophisticated graphical user interface, then PdDroidParty by Chris Mc-Cormick may be for you (Figure 3-1). So far, it is only available for Android, but that may change soon; Dan Wilcox recently posted an early version for iOS, called PdParty. PdDroidParty parses a suitably prepared patch and creates a user interface for it, much like that of Pd. At the time of writing, it doesn't provide sensor input to the patch, but sensors are high on the list of features to be added. PdDroidParty is under active development, and so I won't even try to describe the current state here. Besides, Chris's documentation leaves nothing to be desired. Check it out at *http://droidparty.net/*.

Figure 3-1. Deploying a Pd patch with PdDroidParty

If you are familiar with HTML and JavaScript, then PdWebkitDroid, also by Chris McCormick, is worth a look. Like PdDroidParty, it is for Android only and provides a way of running patches with a sophisticated user interface, but the mechanism for creating the user interface is different. You create the user interface as a form in HTML and hook it up to libpd with JavaScript. This is a powerful idea, but for the time being I consider PdDroidParty a stronger deployment platform for Android. In the long run, however, I expect to see libpd-based extensions for all major browsers that will establish Pd as an audio engine for dynamic web pages, and then the approach of PdWebkitDroid will take off.

All four apps, RjDj, ScenePlayer, PdDroidParty, and PdWebkitDroid, are based on libpd. The original RjDj player predates libpd, and the ScenePlayer app for Android was originally conceived as a test case for libpd, in order to find out how the API would hold up in a complex app. When libpd emerged as a credible way of embedding Pd in mobile apps, the team at Reality Jockey took note and switched their own products over to libpd. The original iOS support for libpd was a byproduct of this conversion.

Creating RjDj Scenes

RjDj has been around since 2008, and the process of creating RjDj scenes has been documented elsewhere (more than once), but only for iOS devices. The appearance of the Android ScenePlayer has introduced just enough additional considerations to merit yet another RjDj tutorial.

The original RjDj app is available for free from the App Store. The Android ScenePlayer is available from the Android Market, and it is also one of the sample projects that come with the Android branch of libpd. Figure 3-2 shows the Android version playing *Atsuke*, a scene by Frank Barknecht that he generously made available for distribution with libpd. Some elements of the user interface are obvious, such as the microphone gain slider and the transport buttons. Less obviously, the square image above the microphone slider serves a dual purpose. It visually represents the current scene, but it also receives touch events that are passed on to the Pd patch at the heart of the scene.

You can record yourself singing along with the scene. This is a fun feature, and the iOS version will let you upload your recordings to the RjDj website and share them with other users. Sadly, the recording feature of the Android version is of limited utility because the audio latency of current Android devices may cause synchronization issues. Some scenes are more affected by this than others. Scenes that pick up ambient sounds and weave them into intriguing soundscapes (such as the amazing *World Quantizer* by Roman Haefeli) may still be good candidates for recording.

Before you start making your own scenes, you may want to take a look at what other people have done. Since the inception of RjDj, scene design has evolved a lot, and recent scenes are lightyears away from early scenes in terms of complexity and usability. Then again, many early scenes distinguish themselves through quirky, off-the-wall ideas.

Figure 3-2. ScenePlayer playing Atsuke by Frank Barknecht

Take a look at a selection and get a sense of what's possible, what works and what doesn't. Some representative scenes are available on the resource page of this book, at *http://shop.oreilly.com/product/0636920022503.do.*

Anatomy of an RjDj Scene

An RjDj scene consists of one main patch and several auxiliary files. The main patch is essentially a regular Pd patch, except for a few RjDj-specific objects and abstractions. Most of these points have been documented elsewhere, but only for iOS. We'll give a brief overview of RjDj scene development, paying special attention to Android-specific issues.

Figure 3-3 shows the contents of a typical RjDj scene. The parent directory must contain the main patch and all its dependencies, as well as some additional files. Its name must end with *.rj*.

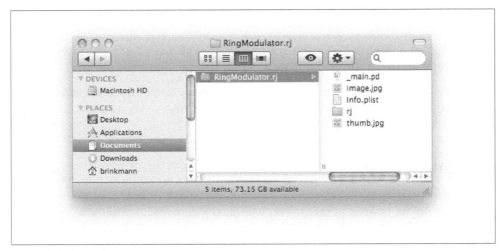

Figure 3-3. Scene directory

_main.pd

    A Pd patch, the heart of an RjDj scene, discussed below.

Info.plist

    Meta-information about the scene. The entries for author, name, and description are required. RjDj also supports a number of optional entries that won't concern us here.

Scene meta-information in XML.

```
<?xml version="1.0" encoding="UTF-8"?>
<!DOCTYPE plist PUBLIC "-//Apple//DTD PLIST 1.0//EN"
"http://www.apple.com/DTDs/PropertyList-1.0.dtd">
<plist version="1.0">
<dict>
    <key>info</key>
    <dict>
        <key>author</key>
        <string>Your name here</string>
```

```
        <key>name</key>
        <string>Scene title here</string>
        <key>description</key>
        <string>Describe the scene here.</string>
    </dict>
  </dict>
  </plist>
```

image.jpg

>   A background image that RjDj will display while playing your scene. It must be a jpeg image 320 by 320 pixels in size.

thumb.jpg

>   An optional thumbnail version of the background image, to be displayed next to the name of your scene. If supplied, it must be a jpeg image 55 by 55 pixels in size.

rj

>   An optional directory containing a collection of abstractions supplied by Reality Jockey Ltd. under the GNU General Public License, discussed below.

RjDj provides a template for new scenes, unsurprisingly named *SceneTemplate.rj*, and it is usually easier to adapt the template to your needs than to create a new scene from scratch.

Patching for RjDj

Patching for RjDj is much like regular patching with Pd, but there are some small but important points to keep in mind. You will need a copy of Pd Vanilla, installed and tested like in Chapter 2, and you will need to configure it for RjDj. You only need to do the configuration once, and then you can leave it in place.

Here are the basic constraints of patching for RjDj.

- Audio parameters are fixed at two input channels, two output channels, and a sample rate of 22050Hz. (Current Android devices only have one microphone, but the ScenePlayer app will duplicate the input channel, so that you can always prepare your patch for stereo input.)
- You can use all objects that come with Pd Vanilla except for adc~, dac~, expr, and expr~.
- Use soundinput instead of adc~, soundoutput instead of dac~.

adc~ and dac~ are, in fact, still available, but the app expects to interact with the patch through soundinput and soundoutput. If you inadvertently use adc~, your scene will appear to work until you try to change the mic volume. If you use dac~, your scene will appear to work until you try to record its output.

Two commonly used externals, `expr` and `expr~`, are missing from the iOS version because they used to be covered by the GNU General Public License, which is incompatible with Apple's App Store. These constraints do not affect Pd itself or the Android ScenePlayer. If you use `expr` or `expr~`, your scene will work with Pd itself as well as the Android ScenePlayer, but it will fail in the original RjDj player.

You will need to download a copy of rjlib, the RjDj development library. Open a terminal, go to the directory where you want to keep your copy of rjlib (e.g., your Documents directory), and clone the library with Git.

```
$ git clone https://github.com/rjdj/rjlib.git
```

You will see a new directory, containing a few files and subdirectories including *rjlib/pd*. Launch Pd Vanilla, select "Pd → Preferences → Path...", and add *rjlib/pd* to the search path of Pd. Now open the audio settings of Pd and select a sample rate of 22050Hz. Click on Apply, and you're ready to create RjDj scenes.

In *rjlib/examplescenes*, you'll find a number of sample scenes that are worth studying, as well as some useful documentation. We'll continue with a slight modification of a familiar patch. Figure 3-4 shows the RjDj version of our ring modulator from Chapter 2.

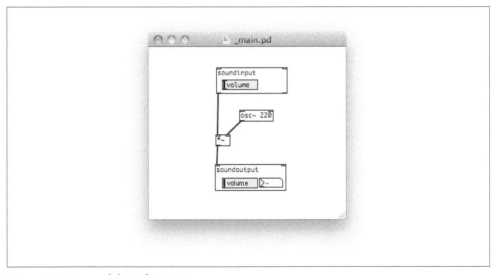

Figure 3-4. Ring modulator for RjDj

Deploying an RjDj Scene

Now that we have a basic scene, let's run it on an actual device. The process of deploying a scene depends on your platform of choice. With Android, it's trivial. Just connect your device to your computer with a USB cable, mount it as a storage device, and copy your entire scene directory to the SD card of the device when it shows up as external storage. After you disconnect the USB cable, you can launch the ScenePlayer app, click on "Install scene from SD card", and select your new scene.

 The ScenePlayer app cannot read your new scene as long as the SD card is mounted on your computer in USB storage mode.

With the RjDj player for iOS, installing a new scene takes more work. For testing and development, you can install Chris McCormick's rjzserver tool on your computer (*http://pure-data.info/rjzserver*). You will also need to configure an HTTP proxy on your iOS device; the *README* file that comes with rjzserver explains how.

When you run rjzserver on your computer, you can point it to a directory containing your scenes, and then it will serve a simple HTML page with installation links (Figure 3-5). Now you point the browser of your iOS device to *http://rjdj.me/* (which will actually resolve to the rjzserver page, due to the HTTP proxy). If you select one of the links, the RjDj app will launch and install the corresponding scene.

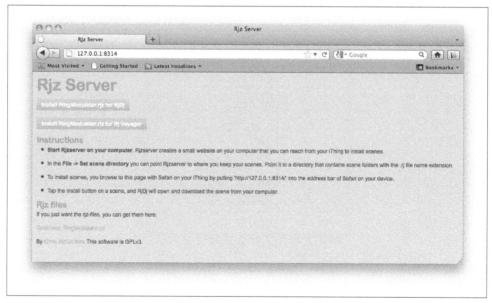

Figure 3-5. rjzserver download window

 On some systems, rjzserver may be thwarted by the firewall or other security features. If you see no response from rjzserver in your browser, take a look at the status window and check for HTTP GET requests (Figure 3-6). If there are no GET requests, you need to adjust your security settings.

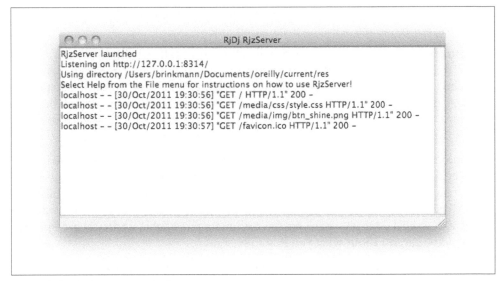

Figure 3-6. rjzserver status window

Scene downloads from rjzserver depend on a custom URI scheme; installation links are of the form *rjdj://host.address/path/scene.rjz*. When you select such a link, the device will look at the scheme of the URI and determine that the RjDj app ought to handle it. Then the RjDj app will take the link, rewrite it as *http://host.address/path/scene.rjz*, and send a regular HTTP GET request to the server. The server will then take the scene directory, package it as a zip file, and send it to the device.

The Android ScenePlayer implements the same URI scheme as the RjDj app, and so you can use rjzserver in order to install scenes on an Android device, although it is usually much easier to copy a scene to the SD card. You won't need to set up an HTTP proxy when using rjzserver with ScenePlayer. Instead, just point your browser to the URL that rjzserver is listening on; it usually looks like *http://192.168.1.1:8314/*, and you can find it in the rjzserver status window (Figure 3-6).

Once a scene is done, you will probably want to share it with other people. Once again, the procedure depends on your platform of choice, and once again it is easier to deploy a scene to Android devices. You simply create a zip file of your scene directory, either by invoking `zip` directly or by downloading it from rjzserver, save it with a *.rjz* extension, and post it on the web with a link using the rjdj URI scheme.

Linking to scenes in rjz format.

```
<html>
  <body>
    <a href="rjdj://your.server.com/path/scene1.rjz">Install Scene 1.</a>
    <a href="rjdj://your.server.com/path/scene2.rjz">Install Scene 2.</a>
  </body>
</html>
```

Now other Android users can install the ScenePlayer app, point the browser of their device to your page, and select an installation link.

Unfortunately, the RjDj app for iOS will refuse to install *.rjz* files from third-party websites. In order to share a scene with iOS users, you can have rjzserver generate an rjz archive for you and upload it to the RjDj website. Their web app will generate an HTML page for your scene, and then other users of the RjDj app can point their browser to your scene page and download the scene from there. Of course, you need to familiarize yourself with their license agreement before uploading any content.

The upload procedure is perfectly straightforward and well-documented on their website. Keep in mind, though, that whatever you upload to their website will be available to anyone with the link to your scene, even though you can choose not to publish the link. Moreover, whenever you upload a new version of your scene, it will be available under a new URL. All previous versions will remain available under their respective URLs, so be careful about what you post.

The RjDj website will refuse to serve *.rjz* files to the ScenePlayer app, and so you cannot reach Android users this way. If you want to make your scene available to users of both platforms (and you should!), then you need to deploy it twice, through RjDj for iOS and through some other website for Android. This is getting confusing, and so we'll sum up deployment options in Table 3-1.

Table 3-1. Scene deployment matrix

	local (SD card)	local (rjzserver)	remote (RjDj site)	remote (other website)
RjDj app	–	+	+	–
ScenePlayer	+	+	–	+

Receiving Sensor Input

Smart phones come with a wide array of sensors: accelerometers, cameras, gyroscopes, microphones, touch screens, etc. All of them are potentially useful for musical expression; this is one of the reasons why mobile devices are such an exciting platform for musical apps. Both the RjDj app and the Android ScenePlayer read input from a number of commonly available sensors and make it available to Pd.

The player apps send touch and accelerometer data to the patch through a pair of receive symbols, #touch and #accelerate. Accelerometer messages are lists of three numbers, representing the coordinates of the current acceleration vector measured in multiples of Standard Gravity, $g_0 = 9.81 \text{m/s}^2$. Figure 3-7 shows how the coordinate axes relate to the orientation of the device. The axes form a right-handed coordinate system, with the x-axis pointing to the right, the y-axis pointing up, and the z-axis pointing toward the user.

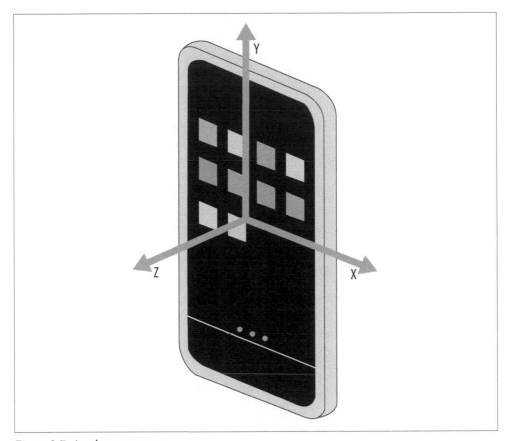

Figure 3-7. Accelerometer axes

The coordinates and units of the acceleration vector are chosen according to the conventions of iOS. Android orients its coordinate system differently and measures acceleration in meters per second squared. The ScenePlayer app automatically transforms acceleration data to the iOS format, so that patches will receive the same kind of data on both platforms.

Keeping track of axes and signs and units can be confusing, but most of the time there is no reason to work with raw accelerometer data. What the accelerometer really gives you is pitch, roll, and magnitude. Pitch and roll provide partial information about the orientation of the device in space. The overall magnitude of the acceleration vector is useful for detecting whether the user is shaking the device. The rjlib library contains abstractions that will compute pitch, roll, and magnitude for you ("Using rjlib" on page 39).

Unfortunately, the accelerometer cannot fully determine the orientation of the device because the third nautical angle, the yaw, can't be read off from the acceleration. For that, you need a gyroscope. (A compass yields similar information, but in practice the built-in compasses of mobile phones are much less accurate than gyroscopes.) RjDj recently introduced gyroscope support for iOS devices; the Android version will probably follow suit in the not too distant future.

The main image in the scene view (Figure 3-2) receives touch events and passes them on to the patch through the receive symbol #touch. Each touch event is a compound message consisting of a symbol, an index, and two coordinates. The symbol takes one of three values, down, xy, and up, indicating whether the event marks the beginning, middle, or end of a touch gesture. The index, starting at 1, is useful for distinguishing multiple simultaneous events on multitouch devices. The coordinates are simply x and y values ranging from 0 to 319, with the origin at the lower lefthand corner of the image.

Controlling Graphics and Text

RjDj offers two objects, rj_image and rj_text, for displaying images and text on top of the main image of the scene. We briefly discuss rj_image and rj_text in their most basic form here. If you want to use them in your own scenes, however, you should also take a look at the convenience wrappers for images and text that rjlib provides (see "Using rjlib" on page 39).

These objects are best suited for providing basic visual feedback, but if you aren't afraid to implement complex logic in Pd, then you can also combine them with the touch input discussed above and build simple graphical user interfaces. Bérenger Recoules has taken this technique quite far in his recent work at Stereolux. He even created an RjDj scene that's actually a simple video game (Figure 3-8).

The rj_image object takes one creation parameter, the path to the image that it is to display. This path is relative to the root directory of the scene. If the image file resides alongside the main patch in the scene directory, then the path is just the name of the image file (Figure 3-9).

Once an image has been created, it can be controlled with two compound messages, `visible flag(` and `move x y(`. The flag must be either 0 or 1 and sets the visibility of the image; the move message translates the center of the image to the given coordinates. Like touch coordinates, they range from 0 to 319, with the origin in the lower lefthand corner.

In order to superimpose text on top of the main image of the scene, you use rj_text objects. Text objects behave much like image objects, except that their creation argument is the original text to be displayed, and they accept two additional messages, `text label(` and `size n(`, that change the text and the font size, respectively.

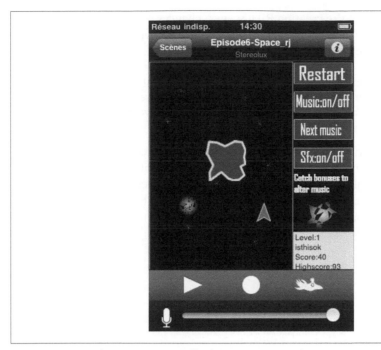

Figure 3-8. RjDj playing Space Traveller by Bérenger Recoules

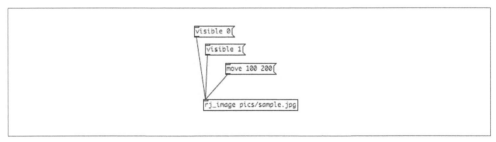

Figure 3-9. Using rj_image

rj_image and rj_text respond to a few other messages, e.g., for changing scale or angle, but those are not part of any official specification and so we won't discuss them here. If you feel like living on the edge, though, you can study the implementation of the Android ScenePlayer to see how they work.

Using rjlib

Let's take a closer look at the rjlib library that we downloaded earlier. So far, we have only used the directory *rjlib/pd*, which contains abstractions like soundinput and soundoutput. The most interesting part of rjlib, however, is the directory *rjlib/rj*, which offers a smorgasbord of useful abstractions. Very few of them are limited to RjDj.

Regardless of whether you're creating RjDj scenes, chances are that you'll find something of interest in *rjlib/rj*. The abstractions in rjlib are the work of Frank Barknecht and Andy Farnell, as well as a number of other contributors.

 Most, but not all, of rjlib is covered by the GNU General Public License. Before you use an abstraction from rjlib, check its license and make sure it is compatible with the licensing and distribution of your work.

The documentation of rjlib is exemplary; it is complete, detailed, and easy to navigate. If you open the file *rjlib/rj/OVERVIEW.pd*, you'll be greeted with a signpost that points to various sections of rjlib (Figure 3-10). If you click on a section, you'll get a list of abstractions in this section. As usual, right-clicking on an abstraction and selecting Help will open a help patch.

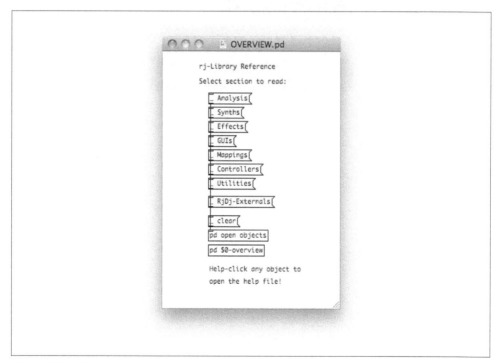

Figure 3-10. rjlib overview

It's a lot of fun to just explore the contents of rjlib for a few hours. Highlights include a drum machine, a Roland Juno-like instrument, an FM emulation of a Rhodes e-piano, resonant filters, and a vocoder. In addition to all this high-level functionality, there is also a large collection of small utilities that solve common problems, such as mappings from raw accelerometer data to pitch and roll.

In order to use rjlib in an RjDj scene, you need to copy the *rj* directory to your scene directory and have *_main.pd* add it to the search path using `declare` objects (Figure 3-11). Now you can use abstractions from rjlib in your patch.

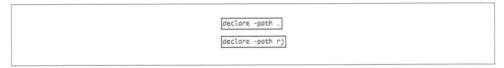

Figure 3-11. Adding rjlib to the search path

Early versions of the RjDj app included a copy of rjlib, and so it wasn't necessary to package a copy of *rj* with a scene. That approach turned out to be too inflexible, however; the update cycle of the app was too slow to keep up with the growth of rjlib. The current approach guarantees that each scene will be deployed with the correct version of rjlib. If you're concerned about the space taken up by rjlib, you can delete unused files. Make sure not to delete too many, though; some abstractions in rjlib depend on other parts of rjlib, and so you may need more than just those files that your patch references directly.

CHAPTER 4

Embedding Pure Data with libpd

Pure Data was originally designed to be an interactive tool for computer music and multimedia, tightly integrating a dataflow programming language and signal processing with a graphical user interface and support for various audio and MIDI interfaces. In this capacity, Pd runs as the top-level application, managing most aspects of its operation and only intermittently delegating control to the audio subsystem of the operating system. The usual way to port Pd to a new platform is by extending Pd, adding support for a new audio API and possibly new objects, known as *externals*, that make special capabilities of the new platform available to Pd.

When I started thinking about porting Pd to Android, I quickly realized that the usual approach wouldn't work. At the time, it was possible for Android apps to have native components written in C, but the main body of an app still had to be written in Java. This restriction has since been lifted, but at the time it was impossible to run an extension of Pd as an Android app. Rather, I had to turn the usual model on its head; instead of extending Pd for a new purpose, I had to find a way to embed Pd into Android apps.

Introducing libpd

After much refactoring, the first prototype of an Android port of Pd fell into five main pieces: Pd itself; a thin wrapper on top of Pd that turns it into an embeddable audio library; Java bindings for this library; some platform-specific glue that ties the Java bindings into the audio architecture of Android and provides some common utilities; and the top-level application code. This structure turned out to be highly versatile and applicable to a range of uses far beyond Android, and virtually all libpd-based applications adhere to the same layer model (Figure 4-1).

In the strictest sense, the term libpd only refers to the second layer (the library wrapper for Pd), but we will play fast and loose with the terminology and include language bindings and audio glue when we talk about libpd.

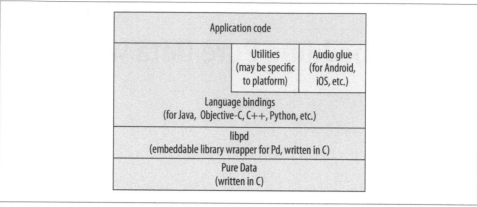

Application code		
	Utilities (may be specific to platform)	Audio glue (for Android, iOS, etc.)
Language bindings (for Java, Objective-C, C++, Python, etc.)		
libpd (embeddable library wrapper for Pd, written in C)		
Pure Data (written in C)		

Figure 4-1. Layer model of libpd development

In this model, each layer only communicates with the layers immediately next to it. Pure Data is written in C, using custom datatypes. The libpd wrapper is also written in C, but its API uses standard datatypes as much as possible. In those few cases where libpd exposes pointers to a Pd-specific datatype, it also provides convenience functions that allow developers to treat those pointers as opaque, without requiring any knowledge of the underlying datatype. The language bindings do away with custom datatypes altogether and exclusively use built-in types of the target language, such as floats, strings, arrays, and lists.

We won't be writing any code in this chapter, but if you want to download a copy of libpd for closer examination, you can open a terminal and say `git clone git://github.com/libpd/libpd.git`. Keep in mind, however, that in subsequent chapters we'll pull in a separate copy of libpd as a submodule of Android or iOS projects. If you clone libpd now, you'll have two copies of it later, and you'll need to be careful not to get them mixed up.

API Overview

In this chapter, we will discuss the parts of libpd that are common to both Android and iOS, up to some minor concessions to language and idiom. Those parts include methods for opening and closing patches, for sending messages to and receiving messages from Pd, and for reading and writing arrays in Pd. That's almost all of libpd, except for the most important parts, the methods that perform the actual audio processing. Musical apps will never call those directly; rather, they will use them by way of platform-specific audio glue.

In both Java and Objective-C, the low-level bindings for libpd are provided by a class called PdBase that is designed to be as small and thin as possible. Its methods are meant to preserve the flavor of old-school C programming that marks Pd itself. In particular, all methods of PdBase are static, and most of them don't throw exceptions; if something goes wrong, they return a nonzero error code. In some cases, it may make sense to create a class that wraps PdBase in a more object-oriented way; this can be useful if you want to mock out the Pd components for testing, or if you want to provide high-level exception handling. Still, in the spirit of minimality, libpd refrains from introducing unnecessary layers of indirection.

All public methods in PdBase are synchronized, providing a basic level of thread safety. In particular, they guarantee that you can use PdBase in a threaded setting without having to worry about crashes due to race conditions or visibility issues. This is an important point because virtually all libpd-based apps will have at least two threads, one for the user interface and one for audio.

 For the vast majority of apps, the synchronization provided by PdBase is all the thread safety you'll need. It is not a silver bullet, however, and concurrency-related issues may still sneak up on you. In particular, if you need to be sure that the state of Pd won't change between subsequent invocations of methods in PdBase, you have to consider additional synchronization.

Opening Patches

Opening patches in Java.

```
static int openPatch(File file) throws IOException;
static int openPatch(String path) throws IOException;
static void closePatch(int handle);
```

Opening patches in Objective-C.

```
+(void *)openFile:(NSString *)baseName path:(NSString *)pathName;
+(void)closeFile:(void *)handle;
+(int)dollarZeroForFile:(void *)handle;
```

The calls for opening and closing patches differ slightly between Java and Objective-C, but the basic behavior is the same. You open a patch by sending the path to the patch to libpd, and you get back a handle that identifies the patch. When you want to close the patch, you pass its handle to the close method. You can open multiple copies of the same patch and tell them apart by their handles.

In Objective-C, the handle is simply a pointer to the data structure that represents the patch in Pd, but you can treat it as an opaque pointer in your application code. If you pass this pointer to dollarZeroForFile, you will get the $0 tag of the topmost patch in your file.

As we saw in Chapter 2, the $0 tag is a unique identifier that Pd assigns to a patch, and it is frequently used when creating symbols that are local to a patch. In Java, we can't use pointers to refer to a patch, and so the openPatch methods in the Java version of PdBase simply return the $0 tag as a handle. Unlike the rest of PdBase, the openPatch methods in Java will throw an exception if something goes wrong.

You don't have to worry about initializing libpd; the first time you call a method in PdBase, libpd will be initialized automatically.

Finding Resources

Setting the search path in Java.

```
static void clearSearchPath();
static void addToSearchPath(String path);
```

Setting the search path in Objective-C.

```
+(void)clearSearchPath;
+(void)addToSearchPath:(NSString *)path;
```

If your patch uses additional resources, such as wav files or abstractions, then it is good practice to package those resources with your patch and to refer to them by relative paths only. In some situations, however, you may have to keep some resources separate from your patch. In this case, you need to add their locations to the search path of Pd so that Pd will be able to find them.

 You may be aware that Pd has two search paths, the regular one and the *extra path*. The extra path exists to solve a problem that won't occur when working with libpd, and so libpd just leaves it blank.

Sending Messages to Pd

Sending messages in Java.

```
static int sendBang(String receiver);
static int sendFloat(String receiver, float value);
static int sendSymbol(String receiver, String symbol);
static int sendList(String receiver, Object... list);
static int sendMessage(String receiver, String message, Object... list);
```

Sending messages in Objective-C.

```
+(int)sendBangToReceiver:(NSString *)receiverName;
+(int)sendFloat:(float)value toReceiver:(NSString *)receiverName;
+(int)sendSymbol:(NSString *)symbol toReceiver:(NSString *)receiverName;
+(int)sendList:(NSArray *)list toReceiver:(NSString *)receiverName;
+(int)sendMessage:(NSString *)message withArguments:(NSArray *)list
        toReceiver:(NSString *)receiverName;
```

Sending messages to Pd is perfectly straightforward. For each supported message type (bang, float, symbol, list, typed message), there is a method that sends a message to a receive symbol in Pd. For instance, in order to send a pitch value of 72 to our synthesizer patch from Chapter 2, we would say `PdBase.sendFloat("midinote", 72)` in Java, or `[PdBase sendFloat:72 toReceiver:@"midinote"]` in Objective-C.

The elements of list or typed messages must be strings or numbers, i.e., they must be of type `String`, `Integer`, `Float`, or `Double` in Java, and `NSString` or `NSNumber` in Objective-C. The return value is an error code that will be nonzero if something went wrong, e.g., if the given receiver does not exist or if list objects are of the wrong type. Failures of send methods are rare and usually benign, and so most apps will just ignore their return values.

libpd supports all message types in Pd except pointer messages. The omission of pointer messages was deliberate because Pd pointers have no semantics outside of Pd itself. If you need your app to interact with pointers in Pd, you can store them in a pointer object in your patch and trigger them with a bang from libpd.

Receiving Messages from Pd

Receiving messages from Pd requires several steps. First we need to create a receiver class that implements callbacks for handling messages from Pd, then we register an instance of this class with libpd, and finally we let libpd know which send symbols in Pd we want to subscribe to. This quickly leads to repetitive code, especially when we are receiving messages from multiple send symbols in Pd, and so we won't discuss the general approach in detail.

Instead, we'll focus on a special case, a utility class that encapsulates the routine aspects of handling messages from Pd and lets the developer focus on the interesting bits. This utility class, `PdDispatcher`, is included in the distribution of libpd, for both Java and Objective-C. It implements a publisher-subscriber (pub/sub) pattern for routing messages from Pd.

In order to receive messages from Pd, we register an instance of `PdDispatcher` with libpd. For each send symbol in Pd that we're interested in, we register one or more listeners with the dispatcher; the listeners implement callback methods that are ultimately responsible for handling events from Pd (Figure 4-2). Behind the scenes, the dispatcher will subscribe to messages from those send symbols. When a Pd message is sent to one of those symbols, the dispatcher will look up the associated listeners and invoke their callback methods for this type of message.

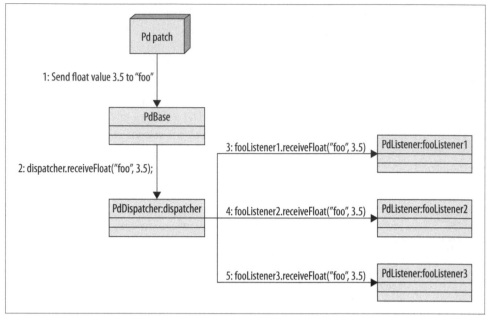

Figure 4-2. Pub/sub messaging with PdDispatcher

Setting up PdDispatcher in Java.

```
PdDispatcher dispatcher = new PdUiDispatcher();
// Note that we're instantiating a subclass, PdUiDispatcher,
// for reasons explained later on in the text.
PdBase.setReceiver(dispatcher);
```

Setting up PdDispatcher in Objective-C.

```
dispatcher = [[PdDispatcher alloc] init];
[PdBase setDelegate:dispatcher];
```

The code snippets in the sections Setting up PdDispatcher in Java on page 48 and Setting up PdDispatcher in Objective-C on page 48 create a dispatcher object and register it with `PdBase`. Note that the `setDelegate` method in Objective-C retains the dispatcher object. If you aren't using automatic reference counting (ARC), you're free to call `[dispatcher release]` after you've registered it with `PdBase`. Regardless of whether you're using ARC, you will need to call `[PdBase setDispatcher:nil]` if you want to unregister and release the dispatcher object altogether.

In addition to the message types we already discussed, dispatchers will also handle printing from Pd, i.e., the messages that appear in the main window when you're working with Pd itself. Printing is generally not suitable for sending data from Pd to the application code, but it pays to log what Pd prints because you occasionally get useful debugging output that way.

When working with audio, you need to have some awareness of concurrency issues because audio apps typically have at least two threads, the audio thread and the main thread. (In practice, the operating system may spin off many more threads for each app, but these two are the ones that most developers should know of.) Messages generated by Pd originate from the audio thread, but in the vast majority of cases they will affect the user interface, and so they have to be consumed on the main thread.

The best way to dispatch events to the main thread depends on the platform, and the Android branch of libpd takes a different approach from the iOS branch. Invoking callback methods in Objective-C typically involves some memory allocation, which is slow and may even block for an indeterminate amount of time. In the audio thread, we cannot afford blocking calls, and so in the iOS branch of libpd, the audio thread just writes an efficient binary representation of a Pd message to a lock-free buffer shared by the two threads.

The main thread polls this buffer every 20ms, converts Pd messages to Objective-C datatypes, and invokes message callbacks as needed. Like this, all potentially slow operations occur on the main thread, and the audio thread does as little work as possible. The downside of this approach is that the shared message buffer may fill up if the main thread fails to consume messages in a timely fashion. In most cases, this is an indication that your patch generates messages at an unreasonable rate and needs to be revised, but if you're really determined to send a torrent of messages from Pd to your app, you can try to remedy the occasional overflow by increasing the size of the message buffer. In order to do this, call [PdBase setMessageBufferSize:nBytes] before you install the dispatcher. If you don't explicitly set the buffer size, the setDispatcher method will allocate a default buffer of 32K. Once the buffer has been allocated, further invocations of setMessageBufferSize have no effect.

For Android, the situation is different, for various reasons. One reason is that the Objective-C components of libpd will only be used with iOS and MacOS, and so it makes sense to bake Cocoa-specific optimizations right into PdBase.m. The Java bindings of libpd, on the other hand, are designed for use beyond the scope of Android, and we cannot make Android-specific assumptions about threading at this level. Hence, the Java bindings pay no attention to threads and just invoke message callbacks on the same thread where they also perform their audio processing. Fortunately, this is not much of a concern because object creation is cheap in Java, and so the conversion of Pd messages from C to Java puts little extra strain on the audio thread.

 If you are concerned about placing Java-related overhead on the audio thread, then you can implement your audio components entirely in C, bypassing the Java bindings and using the C API of libpd directly. That would be the topic of another book, though, and besides, it's not clear how much there is to gain. Before you embark on such a project, you probably want to build a quick prototype in Java, profile it, and convince yourself that the expected performance gain will be worth the effort.

While most Pd messages will originate from the audio thread, they are usually meant to affect the user interface. Since most GUI methods can only be invoked on the main thread, most Pd messages need to be handled on the main thread, and that's where the `PdUiDispatcher` class comes in. It's a subclass of `PdDispatcher` that invokes listener callbacks on the main thread. If you use this class, you can implement your message handlers without having to pay any further attention to concurrency issues. We will focus on this approach because it is the appropriate one for most apps.

 There are rare cases where it is advantageous to have a choice as to which thread to execute a callback on. If you need this flexibility, you can instantiate `PdDispatcher` directly instead of using `PdUiDispatcher`, at the cost of having to be aware of threading when handling messages. It can be done, and if you're versed in the dark art of Java concurrency and how it pertains to Android, then you can achieve the desired effect with fairly little code. The ScenePlayer app for Android, for instance, creates and updates its user interface without explicit thread management.

Now, in order to receive messages from send symbols in Pd, we need to implement a listener interface. This interface is quite similar to the message-sending API that we already discussed; the source parameter indicates the send symbol in Pd that the message was sent from. You generally won't explicitly call those methods from your code. Instead, libpd will call them when a message from Pd arrives.

Listener interface in Java.

```
public interface PdListener {
    public void receiveBang(String source);
    public void receiveFloat(String source, float x);
    public void receiveSymbol(String source, String symbol);
    public void receiveList(String source, Object... args);
    public void receiveMessage(String source, String symbol, Object... args);
}
```

Listener interface in Objective-C.

```
@protocol PdListener
@optional
- (void)receiveBangFromSource:(NSString *)source;
- (void)receiveFloat:(float)received fromSource:(NSString *)source;
- (void)receiveSymbol:(NSString *)symbol fromSource:(NSString *)source;
- (void)receiveList:(NSArray *)list fromSource:(NSString *)source;
- (void)receiveMessage:(NSString *)message withArguments:(NSArray *)arguments
            fromSource:(NSString *)source;
@end
```

Most implementations of the listener interface will not need to handle all types of messages. In Objective-C, all methods are optional, and so you are free to pick and choose the methods you want to implement. For convenience, the listener interface in Java comes with an adapter class that achieves the same effect.

Let's assume that we have a class, say SpamListener, that implements this interface for the purpose of receiving messages from the send symbol spam. Now we need to create an instance and register it with the dispatcher.

Registering a listener in Java.

```
SpamListener spamListener = new SpamListener();
dispatcher.addListener("spam", spamListener);
```

Registering a listener in Objective-C.

```
SpamListener *spamListener = [[SpamListener alloc] init];
[dispatcher addListener:spamListener forSource:@"spam"];
```

Behind the scenes, the dispatcher will subscribe to messages for the symbol spam. From now on, messages sent to spam in Pd will be received by our listener. Of course, you can add listeners for other symbols as well as multiple listeners for the same symbol. You can also remove listeners that are no longer needed.

The Objective-C version of PdDispatcher retains each registered listener, i.e., listeners will not be released as long as they haven't been removed from the dispatcher, regardless of whether you're using ARC.

Reading and Writing Arrays in Pd

Read and write access to arrays in libpd is provided by the following three methods. Veteran C programmers will notice that the Java methods mimic the venerable memcpy function of ANSI C.

Accessing Pd arrays in Java.

```
static int arraySize(String name);
static int readArray(float[] destination, int destOffset,
                     String source, int srcOffset, int n);
static int writeArray(String destination, int destOffset,
                      float[] source, int srcOffset, int n);
```

Accessing Pd arrays in Objective-C.

```
+(int)arraySizeForArrayNamed:(NSString *)arrayName;
+(int)copyArrayNamed:(NSString *)arrayName withOffset:(int)offset
            toArray:(float *)destinationArray count:(int)n;
+(int)copyArray:(float *)sourceArray toArrayNamed:(NSString *)arrayName
    withOffset:(int)offset count:(int)n;
```

Most of the time, you will probably want to copy entire arrays, in which case both source and target arrays will be of the same size, the offsets will be zero, and the count n will be the size. In some cases, however, you may only want to work with small regions of a large array, and then you can specify the regions in terms of offset and count.

It is easy to change the size of an array in Pd, and Pd patches do this often. If you are working in a threaded setting, libpd cannot guarantee that the array size will remain the same between invocations of methods of PdBase. All array access methods of PdBase check the bounds of arrays, and so there is no risk of crashes due to mismatched array sizes. Still, the application code will be much easier to write if the sound designer agrees not to resize arrays.

MIDI Support in libpd

Recent versions of libpd support MIDI using an API that's similar to the API for exchanging messages with Pd, consisting of a set of functions for sending MIDI messages to Pd as well as support for receivers that handle MIDI messages from Pd. If you're thinking about using the MIDI capabilities of libpd, though, you should take a moment and ask yourself whether this is really necessary. In many cases, you will be better off using Open Sound Control instead. Support for OSC is provided by externals that are easy to add to any libpd-based app.

As we saw in Chapter 2, there are really only two realistic use cases for MIDI in a mobile musical app. You may want to control external MIDI hardware with your app, or you may want to have your app control a patch that was designed to take its input from a MIDI device.

In the first case, you will be responsible for writing the boilerplate that connects libpd to the MIDI API of your platform (if any). It's not hard, but since this is a rare requirement for mobile apps, we won't discuss it any further.

Shameless plug: If you're developing for Android and you're handy with a soldering iron, then you can build your own Bluetooth-MIDI adapter. You can find links to instructions, schematics, and software on the resource page of this book online, at *http://shop.oreilly.com/product/0636920022503.do*.

The second case may occur if the sound designer chooses to use a MIDI controller when patching for your app. In that situation, the easiest way to deploy the patch is to have the app assume the role of the MIDI controller, and so we need a way to send MIDI events to Pd. Pd and libpd support all MIDI event types; commonly used ones are represented by dedicated objects in Pd and corresponding functions and callbacks in libpd. For the less common event types, Pd and libpd provide access to raw MIDI bytes, although it is not clear whether anyone will ever need this. We'll just list the functions in libpd that send channel voice messages to Pd.

Sending MIDI messages in Java.

```
static int sendNoteOn(int channel, int pitch, int velocity);
static int sendControlChange(int channel, int controller, int value);
static int sendProgramChange(int channel, int value);
static int sendPitchBend(int channel, int value);
static int sendAftertouch(int channel, int value);
static int sendPolyAftertouch(int channel, int pitch, int value);
```

Sending MIDI messages in Objective-C.

```
+(int)sendNoteOn:(int)channel pitch:(int)pitch velocity:(int)velocity;
+(int)sendControlChange:(int)channel controller:(int)controller value:(int)value;
+(int)sendProgramChange:(int)channel value:(int)value;
+(int)sendPitchBend:(int)channel value:(int)value;
+(int)sendAftertouch:(int)channel value:(int)value;
+(int)sendPolyAftertouch:(int)channel pitch:(int)pitch value:(int)value;
```

Most of the parameters are unsigned 7-bit integers, i.e., their values range from 0 to 127. The only exceptions are channel numbers and pitch bend values. Those two tend to cause some confusion because their binary representation in the MIDI wire format differs from their musical interpretation. Even worse, the pitch bend objects in Pd are inconsistent in their interpretation of pitch bend values.

We resolve this problem by choosing sanity over MIDI specs or consistency with Pd. To wit, channel numbers range from 0 to 15 as far as libpd is concerned, and pitch bend values range from -8192 to 8191, with 0 representing neutral pitch bend. In other words, parameters behave the way a programmer would expect them to, and libpd handles any conversions behind the scenes.

Odds and Ends

When your app is done with Pd, you should release the resources held by libpd. While it's always a good idea to free up resources as soon as you don't need them anymore, calling `PdBase.release()` is critically important for certain Android apps, for reasons we'll discuss in Chapter 5. When working in Objective-C, you should close all patches and release the dispatcher object by calling `[PdBase setDispatcher:nil]`.

This completes the list of methods in `PdBase` that you will commonly use when making musical apps. If you take a close look at the class definition, however, you will find a few more methods. Some of them are there for completeness but are rarely needed; the rest are used by the audio glue and will not be called by application code.

Externals in libpd

The functionality of Pd is commonly enhanced by the addition of externals, i.e., objects that are not built into Pd but loaded at runtime, as needed. In fact, many users of Pd do not use Pd Vanilla but Pd Extended, which comes with a wide range of additional externals that provide many useful features.

Patching for libpd tends to involve fewer externals than patching for Pd itself. One reason is that many externals enhance the user interface of Pd, which libpd discards. Another reason is that with libpd, you don't always have to use an external if you need additional functionality. In many cases, it is easier to implement the desired functionality in your application code instead.

If you want to use externals with libpd, however, you can, both with Android and iOS. The details are highly platform-dependent, and so we will discuss them in Chapter 5 and Chapter 6.

 Unlike the core of Pd and libpd, which have been released under a BSD license, many externals are covered by the GNU General Public License or the GNU Lesser General Public License. Surprisingly, that includes two of the externals that come with Pd Vanilla, expr and expr~. This is an important concern to keep in mind, especially if you intend to submit your app to Apple's App Store. If you're thinking about using externals in your app, check their licenses and make sure that they are compatible with the license of your app.

Audio Glue

The audio architectures of Android and iOS are quite different, but libpd aims to provide a coherent interface across platforms, without sacrificing platform-specific functionality. We discuss the common features here and leave most platform-specific considerations for Chapter 5 and Chapter 6.

The common features of the audio glue include methods for initializing, starting, and stopping the audio components, as well as a method that checks whether the audio components are currently active. In Java, the audio glue is provided by a class called PdAudio; in Objective-C, a class called PdAudioController plays a similar role.

Audio glue in Java.

```
public class PdAudio {
  static void initAudio(int sampleRate, int inChannels, int outChannels,
                        int ticksPerBuffer, boolean restart) throws IOException;
  static void startAudio(Context context);
  static void stopAudio();
  static boolean isRunning();
}
```

Audio glue in Objective-C.

```objc
@interface PdAudioController : NSObject <AVAudioSessionDelegate>

@property(nonatomic, readonly) int sampleRate;
@property(nonatomic, readonly) int numberChannels;
@property(nonatomic, readonly) BOOL inputEnabled;
@property(nonatomic, readonly) BOOL mixingEnabled;
@property(nonatomic, readonly) int ticksPerBuffer;

@property (nonatomic, getter=isActive) BOOL active;

-(PdAudioStatus)configurePlaybackWithSampleRate:(int)sampleRate
                            numberChannels:(int)numChannels
                             inputEnabled:(BOOL)inputEnabled
                           mixingEnabled:(BOOL)mixingEnabled;

-(PdAudioStatus)configureAmbientWithSampleRate:(int)sampleRate
                           numberChannels:(int)numChannels
                          mixingEnabled:(BOOL)mixingEnabled;

-(PdAudioStatus)configureTicksPerBuffer:(int)ticksPerBuffer;

@end
```

---

libpd and Core Audio

If you are familiar with Core Audio in iOS, then you may have noticed that the configuration options of `PdAudioController` neatly map to audio session categories. To wit, the `configurePlaybackWithSampleRate` method will choose either `AVAudioSessionCategoryPlayAndRecord` or `AVAudioSessionCategoryPlayback`, depending on whether audio input is required. The `configureAmbientWithSampleRate` method will choose `AVAudioSessionCategoryAmbient` or `AVAudioSessionCategorySoloAmbient`, depending on whether mixing is enabled. The configuration options give access to all session categories that make sense for libpd, at least according to Apple's documentation. In practice, some configurations may not be available on your target device. Make sure to test your code on an actual device and be prepared to try more than one audio configuration.

The mixing flag indicates whether the audio session will allow simultaneous output from other apps. Moreover, an instance of `PdAudioController` will register itself as an audio session delegate that suspends audio playback when a phone call comes in.

The goal of `PdAudioController` is to encapsulate commonly used behavior in order to protect developers from having to worry about configuration details of Core Audio. If the default behavior of `PdAudioController` does not meet your needs, you can create a subclass that overrides the methods that you wish to modify.

As a matter of fact, `PdAudioController` is merely a utility class that configures the audio session and then runs Pd in an audio unit provided by another class, `PdAudioUnit`. If you find `PdAudioController` entirely unsuitable, you can bypass it altogether and use `AVAudioSession` together with `PdAudioUnit` in order to gain complete control of your audio setup.

In order to initialize the audio glue, you need to specify a number of parameters. Most of them (sample rate, number of channels) are obvious, but one, the number of ticks per buffer, requires an explanation.

Pd computes audio in chunks of 64 frames, known as *ticks*. When specifying the number of ticks per buffer, you are effectively choosing the duration of the audio buffer through which Pd will exchange audio samples with the operating system. For example, if you request four ticks per buffer at a sample rate of 44100Hz, then the duration will be 4 * 64 / 44100Hz = 5.8ms. Note that this is only a request; `PdAudio` and `PdAudioCon troller` will negotiate with the audio subsystem to get a buffer size that's as close as possible to your request, but depending on the capabilities of your platform, the actual buffer size may be different.

In Objective-C, you don't have to explicitly specify the number of ticks per buffer because Core Audio will provide a usable default: If you don't set the number of ticks per buffer, the buffer size will be 512 frames, i.e., eight ticks per buffer.

One minor difference between the Android version and the iOS version is that the Android version will let you choose any combination of input and output channels as long as the requested channel numbers are available, while most audio configurations for iOS will only allow audio output. When audio input is enabled, the number of input channels must equal the number of output channels because the audio unit that connects libpd to Core Audio uses the same channel configuration and buffer for both input and output.

Another difference is the way `PdAudio` and `PdAudioController` handle configuration failures. In Java, `PdAudio` will either give you the configuration you requested, or it will fail and throw an `IOException`. In Objective-C, the configuration method returns a value of type `PdAudioStatus`, which is an enum with three elements: `PdAudioOK`, `PdAudio Error`, and `PdAudioPropertyChanged`. The first two indicate success or failure, as one might expect. The third one, `PdAudioPropertyChanged`, indicates partial success, i.e., the controller was able to configure the audio session and create an audio unit, but it had to adjust some parameters. For example, if the requested sample rate is not available, the controller will use the current hardware sample rate instead. When asked to configure input channels on a system that does not provide audio inputs, the controller will configure the audio without inputs. If an audio configuration method returns `PdAudioPropertyChanged`, you can query the properties of the controller in order to determine whether the outcome is acceptable, or you can just treat it as a failure.

Not only does the audio glue protect you from having to deal with the complexity of the audio subsystem, it also lets your app benefit from the evolution of the underlying technology. You specify the buffer size (essentially, the latency) that you want, and `PdAudio` and `PdAudioController` will get you as close to that as currently possible.

Once the audio glue has been initialized, all you need to do is activate and deactivate it as needed. In Java, this is accomplished by calling `startAudio` and `stopAudio`. In Objective-C, a setter for the `active` property serves the same purpose. Finally, if you want to change the audio settings, you can call `PdAudio.initAudio(…)` again (make sure to set the `restart` parameter to `true`) or reconfigure your instance of `PdAudioControl ler`. Keep in mind, however, that some patches configure themselves at load time, and they may malfunction if you change the sample rate after they have been loaded.

 In Chapter 2, I mentioned that the DSP toggle of Pd is redundant when working with libpd. Now we see why. With libpd, it is preferable to start or stop the audio thread instead of toggling the DSP state of Pd. Using two controls for the same purpose would be a recipe for confusion. `PdAudio` and `PdAudioController` will automatically enable DSP in Pd upon initialization; I strongly recommend that you don't touch the DSP toggle of Pd, neither in your patch nor in your application code.

In both Java and Objective-C, the methods for starting and stopping the audio thread simply turn audio processing on and off. This can result in discontinuities in the sound, which will be audible as clicks. The basic audio glue makes no attempt to avoid clicks because there are many different ways of dealing with clicks, and different apps will have different requirements. If clicks on start or stop turn out to be a concern for you, you are responsible for dealing with them. A common technique is to ramp the audio output down before stopping the audio thread, and then ramp it back up when starting the thread again; you can implement this in a subclass of `PdAudio` or `PdAudioControl ler`. Miller Puckette's book, *The Theory and Technique of Electronic Music*, discusses clicks and their suppression in great depth.

Launch Sequence

When initializing a libpd-based app, it is important to perform the setup in the correct order. Most apps should stick to the following sequence:

1. Initialize the audio components.
2. Create a dispatcher and register it with `PdBase`.
3. Add listeners, if any.
4. Load your patch or patches.
5. Start the audio components.

This order is not cast in stone. The most important rule is that you should initialize the audio components before you open any patches because some patches will query Pd for audio properties like the sample rate upon loading. Everything else is flexible, and you can disregard even this rule if you know that your patches will not query audio properties on load.

Still, it's a good idea to register a dispatcher early on, even if you don't intend to add any listeners, because it will log console message from Pd that may give you useful debugging information. You can add or remove listeners at any time, but if you open patches before your listeners are in place, you may miss messages from Pd.

Also, as long as your audio is initialized, you can open or close patches at any time, but if you load a large patch while another patch is playing, you may get audio dropouts. Then again, some developers have created apps that open lots of patches on the fly without ill effects, while the audio thread is running. Don't be afraid to experiment.

CHAPTER 5

Pd for Android

Android audio development poses some unique challenges. Before you start making a musical app for Android, you have to consider the limitations of the platform. The biggest problem is latency; at the time of writing, round-trip latency for audio I/O is in the hundreds of milliseconds on all devices that I know of (fortunately, straight output latency is significantly lower). Another concern is fragmentation. The Android ecosystem has many niches, populated by a bewildering array of devices covering a wide range of OS versions, screen sizes, and input methods, frequently complicated by manufacturer-specific tweaks to the software. Audio capabilities and computing power vary widely as well, and it is not easy to discover the audio properties of a given device.

Don't be discouraged, though. After all, libpd itself got its start as an Android project, and the open nature of Android makes it a delightful platform to develop for. The good news is that if you can live with the latency, then libpd will provide ready-made solutions or workarounds for most of the other concerns. For instance, the `Audio Parameters` class that comes with libpd employs various tricks to get the device to reveal its audio capabilities. The `PdAudio` class that we already saw in Chapter 4 delegates to another class, `AudioWrapper`, which provides a reasonable approximation of synchronized input and output and also papers over some known, device-specific issues. If you decide that libpd is not for you but you still want to do audio with Android, then you may want to take a look at `AudioParameters` and `AudioWrapper` anyway.

Generally speaking, the audio glue of libpd will deal with much of the platform-specific complexity for you. Even better, it will track the development of Android as the platform evolves, and if a future revision allows for lower latency, your app will automatically reap the benefits, without requiring any changes to your code.

While libpd aims to be as general as possible, supporting Android versions as old as 1.5, I recommend that you take advantage of Android Market filters to limit your apps to the narrowest segment that you can get away with. Unless you have a very compelling reason to aim lower, you should require at least Android 2.2 (which introduced a just-in-time compiler to great effect) and an ARMv7 processor.

Don't feel bad about excluding owners of obsolete or underpowered devices. They'll be disappointed one way or another, but if you let them use your app first, you're risking bad reviews.

Setting Up the Development Environment

Before you do anything else, please double-check that the prerequisites listed in Chapter 1 are in place. You will need a working Android development environment, using ADT Version 15 or later, Java 1.6 and Eclipse 3.7 or later, as well as an installation of Git and some basic working knowledge of the Unix command line (which may take the form of GitBash if you're using Windows).

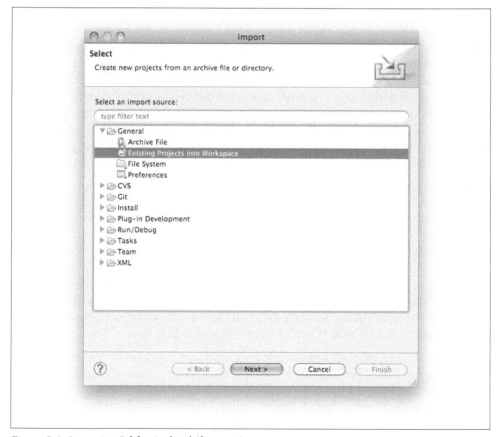

Figure 5-1. Importing Pd for Android (first step)

In order to download a copy of the Android branch of libpd, open a terminal (GitBash under Windows), cd into the directory where you want to keep your installation of libpd (this directory must not be in your Eclipse workspace directory), and enter the following commands:

```
$ git clone git://github.com/libpd/pd-for-android.git
$ cd pd-for-android
$ git submodule init
$ git submodule update
```

This will install libpd and its audio glue for Android, as well as a number of sample apps. Now open Eclipse and select "File → Import...". In the import dialog, select "General → Existing Projects into Workspace" (Figure 5-1). Select your *pd-for-android* directory as the root directory and click on Finish (Figure 5-2). Eclipse will import all projects under your *pd-for-android* directory into its workspace. In most cases, this will complete your setup for Android development with libpd.

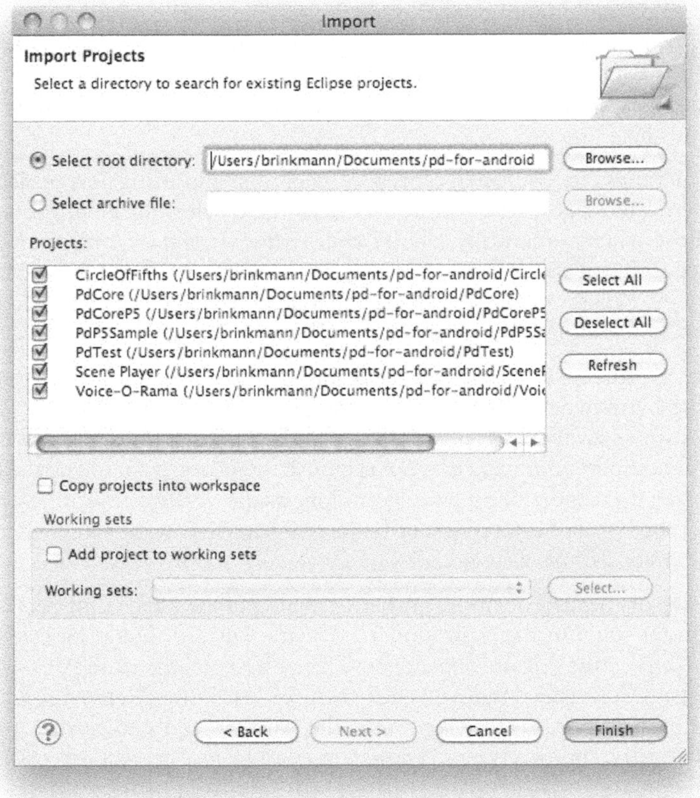

Figure 5-2. Importing Pd for Android (second step)

If you experience trouble when importing projects, you may be tempted to edit the code to address error messages, or to change the Java build path to include dependencies that Eclipse claims are missing. *Resist that temptation.* Those errors are entirely spurious; all projects in Pd for Android come properly configured. Any initial failures should be addressed using the techniques discussed in the section "Fun and Games with Eclipse" on page 62.

The good news is that most problems of this kind are confined to the initial import. Once the sample projects are up and running, it is usually smooth sailing. If you should run into trouble later, possibly after updating your copy of the Android Development Tools, try opening the context menu of your project and selecting Android Tools→Fix Project Properties. This will frequently resolve configuration problems.

Fun and Games with Eclipse

When developing Android apps with Eclipse, you will occasionally run into bugs and quirks that have nothing to do with your code. The most common problem is that Eclipse tends to let its internal state go stale, and then it is up to the developer to recognize this condition and to remedy it through a sequence of refreshing, cleaning, and rebuilding operations. We'll briefly discuss the most common failures and their workarounds here.

Eclipse sometimes gets confused, especially when first importing new projects. If you see bogus error messages, select Project → Clean and try cleaning all projects. If you're lucky, Eclipse will automatically rebuild your entire workspace, and spurious errors will disappear. If you aren't lucky, you may have to clean and rebuild twice. If you're really unlucky, Eclipse will be so confused that it can't even clean all projects at once. In that case, try cleaning PdCore first.

If you've tried cleaning and rebuilding, starting with PdCore, and you still see errors, or if Eclipse hangs when rebuilding your projects, try restarting Eclipse. If you see complaints about `@Override` annotations, open the project properties and make sure that the Java compiler compliance level is set to 1.6. In theory, it should not be necessary to specify the Java version for each project as long as the workspace settings are correct. In practice, there have been reports of build problems that went away when project-specific compiler settings were added.

If spurious errors persist, open the properties dialog of the affected project and select Android on the left. On the right, under Libraries, PdCore should be listed as a dependency. Remove the PdCore dependency, click on Apply, then add PdCore and click on Apply again. It is crucial that you click on Apply each time. Removing and reintroducing a library dependency will prompt the Android tools to rewrite one of the configuration files, and this is often enough to goad Eclipse on to a successful build.

If these incantations don't help, check the libpd wiki at GitHub and see whether your particular problem has been reported before. If none of this helps, feel free to start a new thread in the forum at Pd Everywhere.

It is good practice to keep your copy of libpd up to date by regularly updating both the sample apps and the libpd submodule:

```
$ git pull
$ git submodule update
```

Eclipse caches files and doesn't always notice when files change on disk. Whenever you change a file outside of Eclipse (e.g., by having Git pull the latest revision of libpd from the repository), you need to refresh all your projects in Eclipse.

Of all the projects in Pd for Android, PdCore is the most important one. It is a library project that includes libpd, the audio glue and utility classes for Android, as well as some useful resources. We will discuss the contents of PdCore in detail.

For instant gratification, try running a few of the newly imported projects, e.g., CircleOfFifths and ScenePlayer, on an Android device. These two are also good apps to study because they represent the two ends of the spectrum of libpd-based apps. CircleOfFifths is a simple app, consisting of one activity only, and it shows the bare minimum of code that it takes to make an app with libpd. ScenePlayer, on the other hand, pulls out all the stops and shows how to use all major features in a complex app.

You will need a real Android device if you want to write and test musical apps, ideally a powerful one. The emulator is slow, and it will only do audio at 8000Hz, which is not nearly enough for music.

Creating a Musical App: Part I

Let's create a guitar tuner app. Our first version will be nothing more than a digital tuning fork, emitting reference tones on demand. Think of it as *Hello World!* for libpd.

Importing libpd

Create a new Android project in Eclipse, choose a name and a package name as well as an SDK version, and click on Finish. Now open Project → Properties and select Android in the properties dialog. You will see two areas, one for choosing the build target and one for adding library dependencies. Add PdCore as a *library dependency*.

Eclipse offers at least two other ways of expressing dependencies. You can add source folders to your build path, and you can add entire projects as well. None of this will work with Android libraries, but it may put your project in a weird inconsistent state where the Android tools will fail to build your project even though all dependencies appear to be present in Eclipse. Leave the build path alone when adding Android libraries like PdCore.

Still in the properties dialog, choose an appropriate API version (Figure 5-3) and click Apply. At the time of writing, PdCore requires at least API Level 10 (Gingerbread) for development. If you see errors after importing PdCore, you should check the properties of PdCore and find the current target API version. PdBase, PdAudio, and all the resources of PdCore are now available to your app.

You can choose to target an SDK version that's higher than that of PdCore, but you cannot go lower, even if you intend to deploy your app to older devices. That's okay, though, because the target setting in the properties is really only for *building* your app. For *running* your app, you can choose an earlier SDK version by opening *Android-Manifest.xml* and choosing a smaller minimum version number, e.g.:

```
<uses-sdk android:minSdkVersion="8" />
```

This completes the basic setup of our project. Eclipse will show a warning if the minimum SDK version in the manifest differs from the target version specified in the file *project.properties*, but that's harmless. The section "Supporting Multiple SDK Versions" on page 77 discusses the details of how to support a range of different versions in a single app.

 libpd-based apps require at least API Level 3 (Cupcake) to run, which covers virtually all Android devices found in the wild today. Just because you can deploy apps to old devices doesn't mean you should, though. Devices running Cupcake or Donut are usually underpowered, and they account for a vanishing portion of the market. I generally consider API Level 7 the lowest usable choice. Requiring Level 8 will ensure even better performance while still covering 90% of the market.

Configuring libpd

Now we open *GuitarTunerActivity.java* and write the initialization code, consisting of the installation of a dispatcher and the configuration of the audio glue. We won't be receiving any messages from our patch initially, but it will still be helpful to log print messages from Pd. We'll also include stubs of methods for initializing the user interface and for loading patches.

Guitar tuner activity.

```
public class GuitarTunerActivity extends Activity {

    private static final String TAG = "GuitarTuner";
    private PdUiDispatcher dispatcher;

    @Override
    public void onCreate(Bundle savedInstanceState) {
        super.onCreate(savedInstanceState);
        initGui();
```

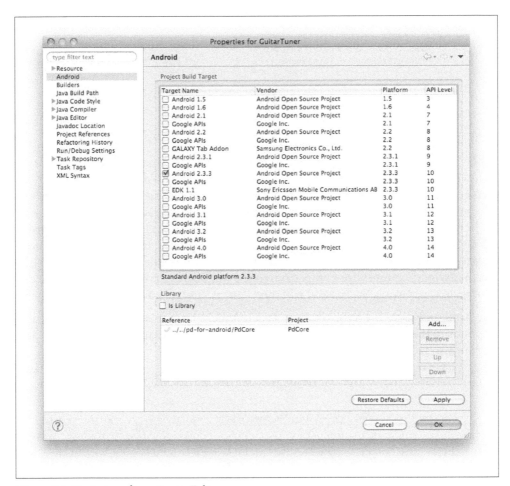

Figure 5-3. Project configuration in Eclipse

```
        try {
            initPd();
            loadPatch();
        } catch (IOException e) {
            Log.e(TAG, e.toString());
            finish();
        }
    }

    private void initGui() {
        setContentView(R.layout.main);
    }

    private void  initPd() throws IOException {
        // Configure the audio glue
        int sampleRate = AudioParameters.suggestSampleRate();
        PdAudio.initAudio(sampleRate, 0, 2, 8, true);
```

```
        // Create and install the dispatcher
        dispatcher = new PdUiDispatcher();
        PdBase.setReceiver(dispatcher);
    }

    private void loadPatch() throws IOException {
        // Stay tuned...
    }
}
```

When configuring the audio glue, we need to keep in mind that we currently have no idea what audio capabilities our device offers. Fortunately, PdCore includes a utility class called AudioParameters that sniffs out available sample rates and channel numbers for you. The first version of our app will use two output channels and no input channels. This channel configuration should be available anywhere, and so we only need Audio Parameters to suggest a sample rate that the device supports. If you want to use more than two channels, you can also ask AudioParameters how many channels are available, but that would be excessive in this case. In the unlikely event that the requested configuration is not available, PdAudio will throw an exception and our app will terminate.

The patch in Figure 5-4 has two controls; a number object that controls the pitch and responds to the receive symbol midinote, and a bang object that triggers the sound and responds to trigger. It's similar to Figure 2-18.

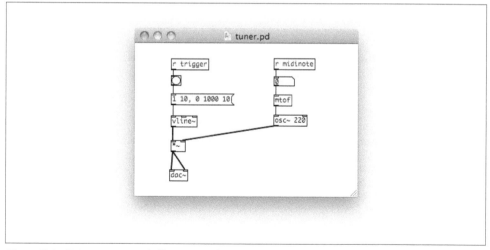

Figure 5-4. Guitar tuner patch (first version)

In order to prepare this patch for deployment, save this patch as *tuner.pd* and package it as a zip file. Move the zip file to the raw resources directory of your Android project (*GuitarTuner/res/raw*) and refresh your project in Eclipse.

Now we implement the `loadPatch` method that was just a stub before. It will unpack the zip file containing our patch into the files directory of our app and then open the patch file:

```
private void loadPatch() throws IOException {
    File dir = getFilesDir();
    IoUtils.extractZipResource(
        getResources().openRawResource(R.raw.tuner), dir, true);
    File patchFile = new File(dir, "tuner.pd");
    PdBase.openPatch(patchFile.getAbsolutePath());
}
```

`IoUtils` is a utility class that comes with libpd and provides commonly used methods for handling files. Pd is not aware of Android resources, and so patches and their associated files have to be written to files before Pd can access them. Packaging the patch as a zip file is not strictly necessary as long as we are only dealing with a single file, but it is good practice anyway, because the above code will still work when our patch grows to include additional files.

 When zipping the patch, be careful not to include the directory containing the patch in your zip file, or else the path of the `patchFile` variable will not be correct. If you prefer to zip your patch by zipping its parent directory, you need to adjust the definition of the `patchFile` variable accordingly.

Now we add code for activating and deactivating the audio glue. The simplest approach is to tie the life cycle of the audio thread to the life cycle of your activity, so that the audio thread will be active whenever the activity is visible:

```
@Override
protected void onResume() {
    super.onResume();
    PdAudio.startAudio(this);
}

@Override
protected void onPause() {
    super.onPause();
    PdAudio.stopAudio();
}
```

We simply start the audio thread in `onResume`, and we stop it in `onPause`. The `start Audio` method needs the application context in order to work around one device-specific bug, and so we pass it the current activity.

In principle, we already have a musical app. If you launch the app now, Pd will load a patch and compute audio samples. Since the patch only renders silence unless prompted, though, you won't hear anything yet. If you want to check whether Pd is already working, you can adjust the patch by adding an oscillator whose outlet is connected to the inlets of `dac~`.

Connecting the User Interface

In order to complete the tuning fork portion of our app, we need to make it interactive. Open *res/layout/main.xml* in Eclipse and add six buttons to your user interface. Set their labels to the names of strings on a guitar, i.e., E, A, D, G, B, and E, and choose their IDs accordingly, say e_button, a_button, etc. Figure 5-5 shows the resulting layout. We use a table layout for the entire user interface because it provides an easy way of laying out our buttons in a grid, and it will be easy to add more widgets later on (see the next code example).

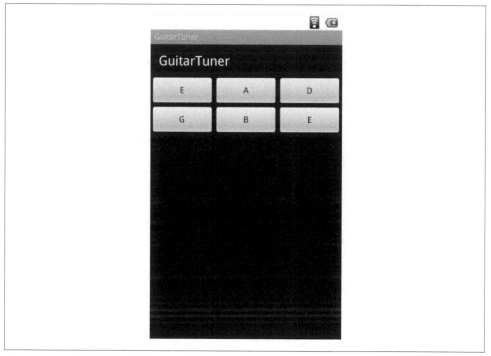

Figure 5-5. User interface (first version)

Adding buttons to the user interface.

```xml
<?xml version="1.0" encoding="utf-8"?>
<TableLayout xmlns:android="http://schemas.android.com/apk/res/android"
    android:layout_width="fill_parent" android:layout_height="fill_parent"
    android:shrinkColumns="*" android:stretchColumns="*">
    <TableRow android:layout_width="fill_parent">
        <TextView android:layout_span="3" android:layout_width="fill_parent"
            android:text="GuitarTuner" android:id="@+id/titleView"
            android:textAppearance="?android:attr/textAppearanceLarge"
            android:layout_height="wrap_content" android:padding="20px"></TextView>
    </TableRow>
    <TableRow android:layout_width="fill_parent">
        <Button android:id="@+id/e_button" android:text="E"></Button>
```

```
    <Button android:id="@+id/a_button" android:text="A"></Button>
    <Button android:id="@+id/d_button" android:text="D"></Button>
  </TableRow>
  <TableRow android:layout_width="fill_parent">
    <Button android:id="@+id/g_button" android:text="G"></Button>
    <Button android:id="@+id/b_button" android:text="B"></Button>
    <Button android:id="@+id/ee_button" android:text="E"></Button>
  </TableRow>
</TableLayout>
```

In order to wire them up, add six fields of type Button to your activity, say eButton, aButton, etc., and initialize them in the initGui method.

```
eButton = (Button) findViewById(R.id.e_button);
eButton.setOnClickListener(this);
aButton = (Button) findViewById(R.id.a_button);
aButton.setOnClickListener(this);
// And so on...
```

After you add these lines, Eclipse will complain that the arguments of setOnClick Listener are of the wrong type. We fix this by having our activity implement the OnClickListener interface.

```
private void triggerNote(int n) {
    PdBase.sendFloat("midinote", n);
    PdBase.sendBang("trigger");
}

@Override
public void onClick(View v) {
    switch (v.getId()) {
    case R.id.e_button:
        triggerNote(40); // E is MIDI note 40.
        break;
    case R.id.a_button:
        triggerNote(45); // A is MIDI note 45.
        break;
    // And so on... The remaining pitch values are 50, 55, 59, and 64.
    }
}
```

This event handler will be called when you click on one of the buttons, and then it will set the desired pitch and trigger a sound. When you run the app and click on the buttons, you'll hear the corresponding notes. You may need to plug in headphones if your built-in speakers are unable to render low frequencies.

 If the audio produced by the app seems noisy, chances are that some other app, most likely your media player, has added audio effects to the global audio session. If this happens to you, open your media player app and check its effects settings. The output of libpd is pristine, but audio effects like BassBoost amplify certain frequency ranges that may come across as noise.

Android API Level 9 added audio effects to the media framework, and libpd provides limited support for the newly introduced audio sessions. Specifically, you can call `PdAudio.getAudioSessionId()` and then use the return value to add equalizers and other effects to your signal processing chain. Generally speaking, though, it is not clear that a libpd-based app has much to gain from additional signal processing outside of Pd. Android audio effects are supported for completeness, but I doubt that they'll see much use with libpd.

If touch sounds are enabled on your device, then Android will acknowledge each button click with a little sound effect. This is rarely the desired behavior for musical apps, and so Pd for Android provides a theme that disables all UI sound effects by globally setting the attribute `android:soundEffectsEnabled` to false. In order to set this theme for your entire app, just add the XML attribute `android:theme="@style/DisableSoundEffects"` to the application tag of your Android manifest:

```
<application android:icon="@drawable/icon" android:label="@string/app_name"
             android:theme="@style/DisableSoundEffects">
```

If you only want to disable sound effects for selected activities, you can add this theme attribute to the appropriate activity tags instead.

Cleaning Up

 If you're wearing headphones, take them off before performing the next step; we're about to experience a horrific glitch.

Leave your app with the Back button and start it again. If you click on the buttons now, you'll hear a badly distorted sound. What's going on here?

We've encountered a most unfortunate interaction between Android and Pd. Process management in Android is unusual in that it leaves little control to the developer. If you leave an activity with the Back button, the activity will be destroyed, but Android may keep its process alive until it needs to reclaim the memory. The goal is to minimize startup times, and that's a good idea in most cases. In our case, however, it runs head-on into the main shortcoming of Pd. Currently, Pd does not admit multiple instances. Instead, there is one global instance of Pd, and this instance holds lots of global state. (I'm lobbying hard to have that fixed.)

When Android keeps the process of our app after the activity finishes, it also keeps Pd with all its state, including our patch. When we launch our app again, it loads the patch again, so that we now have two copies. Their combined output causes the distortion. If you finish and restart the app once more, you'll have three copies of the patch, causing even worse distortion. The solution is to clear the state of Pd when the activity is destroyed:

```
@Override
public void onDestroy() {
    super.onDestroy();
    PdAudio.release();
    PdBase.release();
}
```

 The release methods can only delete objects that PdBase and PdAudio know about, and that's enough for most apps. It is possible, however, to dynamically create objects in Pd that PdBase won't be aware of. If you are using dynamic patching techniques, for example, you are responsible for cleaning up after yourself. If all else fails, you can nuke your process in your finish method, with System.exit(0). Android development guidelines strongly discourage this practice, though.

Configuration changes are a related concern. By default, if the configuration of your app changes (e.g., if the user rotates the device to a different screen orientation), Android will destroy your current activity and recreate it with the new configuration. This hardly matters in our simple example, but as soon as your app plays continuous sound, you probably don't want interruptions from configuration changes.

If you want to support configuration changes, you can work around this problem by implementing the onConfigurationChanged method and adding the appropriate settings to your manifest, but it usually isn't worth the effort. If you can at all get away with it, I recommend that you avoid configuration changes altogether by fixing one configuration in the manifest:

```
<activity android:name=".GuitarTunerActivity" android:label="@string/app_name"
    android:screenOrientation="portrait">
```

This completes the first version of our app. Clearly, our app has lots of room for improvement, but it serves its purpose: It shows the anatomy of a simple libpd-based app with a minimum amount of code. As an exercise, you may want to try and improve this app. Here are a few topics to think about:

- Sending a float and a bang when playing a sound is somewhat redundant. How can you revise the patch so that a midi note message also acts as a trigger? (Hint: Look up triggers in Pd.)
- The sound is quite boring. Can you replace the osc~ object with something that sounds more interesting? (Hint: Look up the phasor~ object for a quick and dirty change, or read up on audio synthesis techniques and try something more sophisticated.)

Creating a Musical App: Part II

So far, our app is essentially a tuning fork. Let's turn it into an actual guitar tuner that picks up sounds from your guitar and lets you know how far you are from the desired pitch. This will require an object that we haven't seen yet, `fiddle~`. It takes an audio stream and extracts a number of useful features from it, most importantly the dominant pitch, which it sends to its left outlet as a MIDI note value (Figure 5-6).

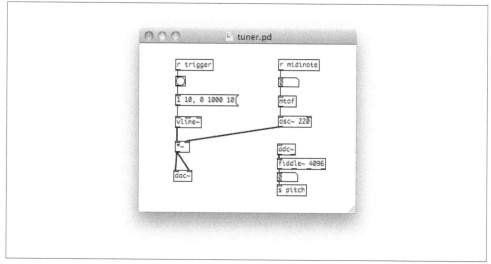

Figure 5-6. Guitar tuner patch (second version)

You can try this in Pd; just open the patch and sing or whistle into the microphone, and you should see note values in the number box that's attached to the `fiddle~` object. Update the zip file containing your patch and don't forget to refresh your project to make Eclipse aware of the change.

Receiving Messages from Pd

We want to read sound input from the microphone now, and so we tell PdAudio to open one input channel for us, in the `initPd` method.

```
PdAudio.initAudio(sampleRate, 1, 2, 8, true);
```

When writing an app for wide distribution, it's a good idea to first ask the `Audio Parameters` class whether audio input is available, but in this tutorial example we'll be content to just have this call fail with an exception if input is not available.

There are cheap off-brand tablets that report that they have a microphone but will fail when asked to open an input channel. So, even if you check audio capabilities with `AudioParameters`, you still need to be prepared to handle failures of `PdAudio`. Moreover, while both the Android API and the libpd API support stereo input, there are currently no Android devices with more than one microphone, and some devices fail silently when asked to provide two input channels. For the time being, it is safer to request no more than one input channel.

Reading input from the microphone is a privileged operation, and so we open *AndroidManifest.xml* and add the permission `android.permission.RECORD_AUDIO`.

In order to receive pitch values from Pd, we register a listener. Since we'll only need to receive one kind of message, we'll derive our listener from the convenient adapter class that's included in the utilities of libpd. For the time being, we just log any values we receive from Pd. Later, when we've verified that this works, we'll display those values in the user interface:

```
dispatcher.addListener("pitch", new PdListener.Adapter()
    @Override
    public void receiveFloat(String source, float x) {
        Log.i(TAG, "pitch: " + x);
    }
});
```

The source parameter of the `receiveFloat` method is redundant in this case, because this listener will only be invoked for messages sent from a single send symbol in Pd; the value of `source` will always be `"pitch"`. In fact, `PdDispatcher` is meant to encourage designs where each listener is attached to one send symbol only, and so it is common for listener implementations to disregard their source parameters altogether. If you find yourself implementing a single listener that checks the source parameter a lot, then you should ask yourself whether it would make sense to refactor it into several listeners, one for each send symbol in Pd.

The adapter class that comes with the `PdListener` interface is convenient, but it is also potential source of subtle bugs. In a properly factored app, a listener ought to be interested in every message sent to its send symbol. If you forget to override a method that's relevant to your app, you won't see any exceptions and unimplemented messages will silently disappear.

Let's launch our app and see what happens. In Eclipse, switch to the DDMS perspective, find the Devices tab, and make sure that your device is selected. You should see output from your app in the logcat tab. If you click on the buttons in the UI, you'll still hear the same sounds as before. Now sing or whistle into the microphone of your device. Do you see any pitch values from Pd in logcat?

Sadly, no. What's wrong? The patch works fine in Pd, we've hooked up the right listener, and we've even remembered to request the appropriate permission. Why aren't we receiving any values from Pd?

If you scroll up in logcat, you'll find a clue to the problem. Just below the system messages that announce the launch of your app, you'll find print output from Pd that tells you that it couldn't create the fiddle~ object.

The reason is that fiddle~ is not a built-in object of Pd but an *external*, i.e., an object that Pd will dynamically load at run-time. Pd Vanilla comes with a number of externals including fiddle~, but libpd will not install them by default because the handling of externals varies greatly from platform to platform. The externals of Pd Vanilla are commonly used objects, though, and so the Android branch of libpd comes with ready-made support for installing them.

Running Pd in a Background Service

The Android branch of libpd includes a class, PdService, that will automatically install the standard externals for you. There are other good reasons for using PdService, too. To wit, if you use PdAudio directly, the way we did when writing the first version of our guitar tuner app, then you basically tie the life of the audio thread to the visible life of one activity. This limitation is unacceptable for many musical apps. For instance, you may want to keep the audio playing in the background when you briefly leave the app in order to read a text message, or maybe you want to create an app that will move between multiple activities without interrupting the audio.

With Android, the solution is to manage the audio thread in a background service that may be shared by several activities and that can remain active in the background even when the app itself is paused. This is the main purpose of PdService; the fact that it also installs the standard externals is merely a convenient side effect.

Let's switch our app from PdAudio to PdService. This will take a fair amount of boilerplate, but if you've worked with background services in Android, the next few steps will be familiar. First we add new fields for the service and for managing the connection to the service:

```
private PdService pdService = null;

private final ServiceConnection pdConnection = new ServiceConnection() {
    @Override
    public void onServiceConnected(ComponentName name, IBinder service) {
        pdService = ((PdService.PdBinder)service).getService();
        try {
            initPd();
            loadPatch();
        } catch (IOException e) {
            Log.e(TAG, e.toString());
            finish();
        }
```

```
        }

        @Override
        public void onServiceDisconnected(ComponentName name) {
            // this method will never be called
        }
    };
```

You'll notice that the onServiceConnected method contains several lines that are familiar from our original onCreate method. That's because the initialization of Pd and the loading of our patch now have to wait until we have a service connection. The new version of onCreate launches the service:

```
    @Override
    public void onCreate(Bundle savedInstanceState) {
        super.onCreate(savedInstanceState);
        initGui();
        bindService(new Intent(this, PdService.class), pdConnection, BIND_AUTO_CREATE);
    }
```

We need to unbind our PdService instance when our app terminates, and we adjust onDestroy accordingly:

```
    @Override
    public void onDestroy() {
        super.onDestroy();
        unbindService(pdConnection);
    }
```

The PdService instance keeps track of its connections, and it will automatically stop the audio thread and clean up after itself when the connection is severed; there's no need to call PdBase.release() or PdAudio.release() here.

In the initPd method, we make a small change that delegates the initialization of the audio glue to the service. The parameters are almost the same as those for PdAudio, except for the buffer size. When initializing PdAudio, we specify the number of ticks per buffer, a somewhat obscure quantity. PdService introduces the additional convenience of letting us specify the desired buffer size in milliseconds. In this case, we ask for 10ms. Keep in mind, though, that this is only a request. The actual buffer will probably be larger, but the good news is that this buffer will automatically shrink as the platform improves. You specify the target latency, and libpd will work hard to get as close to it as possible.

```
    // Configure the audio glue
    int sampleRate = AudioParameters.suggestSampleRate();
    pdService.initAudio(sampleRate, 1, 2, 10.0f);
    pdService.startAudio();
```

Note that we start the audio thread when connecting to the service, and we implicitly stop the audio thread when the onDestroy method unbinds the service. The explicit management of the audio thread in onResume and onPause is no longer necessary, and so we delete both of them. After this step, your code should contain no references to PdAudio anymore. (Do a quick search to confirm this.)

Finally, we need to declare the new service in our manifest.

```
<service android:name="org.puredata.android.service.PdService" />
```

If you run the app now, you'll still hear the same sounds when you click on the buttons. Even better, if you switch to the DDMS perspective in Eclipse and look at the logcat messages, you will see pitch messages sent from Pd. Our service works, and so does our fiddle~ object. Success!

We have, however, incurred a serious usability issue. The life of the audio thread is no longer tied to the visible life of the activity. Rather, the audio thread is launched when the activity connects to the service, and it is only stopped when the activity is destroyed. If you start the app and click on the Back button, the activity will be destroyed and the audio thread with it. If you leave the app by clicking on the Home button, however, the activity will become invisible, but the audio thread will remain active. Since our app will be silent when the user isn't pushing any buttons, it is easy to forget that the audio thread is still running, consuming CPU cycles and draining the battery.

We address this problem by adding a persistent notification to the bar at the top of the screen. As long as our audio thread is active, the user will see a little icon at the top of the screen. Pulling down the bar and clicking on our notification will return to our app. Let's add the following method and call it from the initPd method:

```
private void start() {
    if (!pdService.isRunning()) {
        Intent intent = new Intent(GuitarTunerActivity.this,
                            GuitarTunerActivity.class);
        pdService.startAudio(intent, R.drawable.icon,
                            "GuitarTuner", "Return to GuitarTuner.");
    }
}
```

Now it will be obvious when our app is running in the background, and the notification also guides the user back to our app. As an added benefit, starting our service this way will give it foreground privileges, which increases the odds of it staying alive even when competing for resources with other apps.

At this point, we have performed all the necessary steps to run Pd as a background service, but there is one more usability issue to consider. To wit, it is good practice to pause the audio thread when a phone call comes in. This is not a major concern for our app because it will be silent when nobody is pushing its buttons, but let's see how to implement this anyway.

We need to add one new method and call it from `onCreate`. Monitoring the phone state requires another permission, `android.permission.READ_PHONE_STATE`:

```
private void initSystemServices() {
    TelephonyManager telephonyManager =
        (TelephonyManager) getSystemService(Context.TELEPHONY_SERVICE);
    telephonyManager.listen(new PhoneStateListener() {
        @Override
        public void onCallStateChanged(int state, String incomingNumber) {
            if (pdService == null) return;
            if (state == TelephonyManager.CALL_STATE_IDLE) {
                start();
            } else {
                pdService.stopAudio();
            }
        }
    }, PhoneStateListener.LISTEN_CALL_STATE);
}
```

As I said, a lot of boilerplate. When I write a new musical app, I usually start like we did, using PdAudio directly. If necessary, I switch to PdService, but I don't always monitor the phone state. If there's a risk of interfering with phone calls, I add support for suspending the audio thread when a call comes in.

We are almost done, but we still need to display the output of fiddle~ in our user interface. For now, let's do this in the simplest possible way. First, open *res/layout/ main.xml*, add a text field, and set its ID to pitch_label:

```
<TableRow android:layout_width="fill_parent">
  <TextView android:layout_span="3" android:text="0.0"
    android:id="@+id/pitch_label" android:layout_width="fill_parent"
    android:layout_height="wrap_content" android:padding="20px"></TextView>
</TableRow>
```

Add a field of type TextView to your activity and define it in the initGui method:

```
pitchLabel = (TextView) findViewById(R.id.pitch_label);
```

Go back to your initPd method, delete the original listener that just writes pitch values to logcat, and replace it with a listener that updates our new text field whenever Pd sends a new value. Thanks to the magic of PdUiDispatcher, we don't have to worry about concurrency here. Even though messages from Pd originate on the audio thread, the dispatcher instance will invoke our callbacks on the main thread, and so we can update UI elements without further ado:

```
dispatcher.addListener("pitch", new PdListener.Adapter() {
    @Override
    public void receiveFloat(String source, final float x) {
        pitchLabel.setText("Pitch: " + x);
    }
});
```

If you launch the app now, you'll see a continuous stream of pitch values in the user interface.

Improving the User Interface

While the current version is already enough to illustrate the way libpd handles the communication between Pd and your app, it is not yet terribly useful. After all, the pitch values go by so fast that is hard to read them, and even if we could follow the output, we would still need to know the meaning of MIDI note values by heart in order to make sense of them.

For a more intuitive display, we create a custom view class, PitchView, that shows an analog dial representing pitch values (see the next code example). The new view shows a neighborhood of the target pitch, with the target pitch marked by a green line down the center. If the measured pitch is within a few semitones of the center pitch, a blue line will indicate its current value relative to the center pitch. If it is outside the displayed range, the view will draw a red bar on the left or on the right.

An analog display for pitch values.

```java
public class PitchView extends View {

    private float centerPitch, currentPitch;
    private int width, height;
    private final Paint paint = new Paint();

    public PitchView(Context context) {
        super(context);
    }

    public PitchView(Context context, AttributeSet attrs) {
        super(context, attrs);
    }

    public PitchView(Context context, AttributeSet attrs, int defStyle) {
        super(context, attrs, defStyle);
    }

    public void setCenterPitch(float centerPitch) {
        this.centerPitch = centerPitch;
        invalidate();
    }

    public void setCurrentPitch(float currentPitch) {
        this.currentPitch = currentPitch;
        invalidate();
    }

    @Override
    protected void onSizeChanged(int w, int h, int oldw, int oldh) {
        super.onSizeChanged(w, h, oldw, oldh);
        width = w;
        height = h;
    }

    @Override
    protected void onDraw(Canvas canvas) {
        float halfWidth = width / 2;
        paint.setStrokeWidth(6.0f);
        paint.setColor(Color.GREEN);
        canvas.drawLine(halfWidth, 0, halfWidth, height, paint);

        float dx = (currentPitch - centerPitch) / 2;
        if (-1 < dx && dx < 1) {
            paint.setStrokeWidth(2.0f);
            paint.setColor(Color.BLUE);
        } else {
            paint.setStrokeWidth(8.0f);
            paint.setColor(Color.RED);
            dx = (dx < 0) ? -1 : 1;
        }
```

```
        double phi = dx * Math.PI / 4;
            canvas.drawLine(halfWidth, height,
                halfWidth + (float)Math.sin(phi) * height * 0.9f,
                height - (float)Math.cos(phi) * height * 0.9f, paint);
    }
}
```

The `PitchView` class has two mutable fields, the center pitch and the current pitch, and it offers a pair of accessors for updating them. Graphics programming is beyond the scope of this book, and so we won't discuss the implementation of the `PitchView` class in detail. It is fairly straightforward, though, and a casual reading of the `onDraw` method will give you a good idea of how it works. We now add an instance of `PitchView` at the bottom of our user interface:

```
<TableRow android:layout_width="fill_parent">
  <com.noisepages.nettoyeur.guitartuner.PitchView android:layout_span="3"
    android:layout_width="fill_parent" android:id="@+id/pitch_view"
    android:layout_height="wrap_content">
  </com.noisepages.nettoyeur.guitartuner.PitchView>
</TableRow>
```

With the analog pitch view in place, we need to update our activity to fill the view with life. We will also change the behavior of the `pitchLabel` field. Since we now have a better display of pitch values, we don't need to show raw MIDI note values anymore, and we have the label show the current target pitch instead. In order to give a visual indication that the label has something to do with the center pitch of the analog display, we center the text in our label by adding the attribute `android:gravity="center"` to the pitch label in *main.xml*.

Now, we create a field for the pitch view and initialize it in the `initGui` method:

```
pitchView = (PitchView) findViewById(R.id.pitch_view);
pitchView.setCenterPitch(45);
pitchLabel.setText("A-String");
```

Next, we adjust the listener implementation:

```
dispatcher.addListener("pitch", new PdListener.Adapter() {
    @Override
    public void receiveFloat(String source, final float x) {
        pitchView.setCurrentPitch(x);
    }
});
```

Finally, we change the behavior of our buttons so that they don't just trigger sounds but also set the center pitch of our analog pitch display. If the user triggers a reference tone for a string, the view will automatically be centered on the pitch of the new string, and the label will be updated accordingly. Figure 5-7 shows the user interface of our finished app.

```
private void triggerNote(int n) {
    PdBase.sendFloat("midinote", n);
    PdBase.sendBang("trigger");
    pitchView.setCenterPitch(n);
}

@Override
public void onClick(View v) {
    switch (v.getId()) {
    case R.id.e_button:
        triggerNote(40);
        pitchLabel.setText("E-String");
        break;
    case R.id.a_button:
        triggerNote(45);
        pitchLabel.setText("A-String");
        break;
    // And so on...
    }
}
```

That's it! This simple example has introduced us to all major aspects of developing Android apps with libpd. It also shows how I go about developing a libpd-based app. None of the steps is there for didactic purposes only. If I had written this app by myself, without the intention of explaining how to create a musical app, I still would have proceeded in the exact same way.

The general strategy is to get *something* to work as quickly as possible, and then to arrive at the desired functionality through a sequence of small adjustments, trying each revision as I go along. Even if I know that the app will eventually need to work with PdService, I still start with PdAudio every time because the app will get off the ground more quickly that way. Refining a crude but working app is faster and easier than trying to build a sophisticated app from scratch.

There's still lots of room for improvement. Here are a few ideas:

- While the app is already usable, it still looks quite plain. How would you design a better user interface?
- The fiddle~ object always generates pitch values, even when you aren't playing any notes on your guitar. Modify the patch so that it will only output pitch values for input signals whose volume exceeds a certain threshold. (Hint: In addition to objects that we've already seen, you may want to use threshold~ and spigot.)
- The pitch values seem a bit jittery when you first pluck a string on your guitar. How would you smoothen the pitch values? You might apply signal processing techniques in Pd, or you might have your app interpolate between successive values. What are the trade-offs?

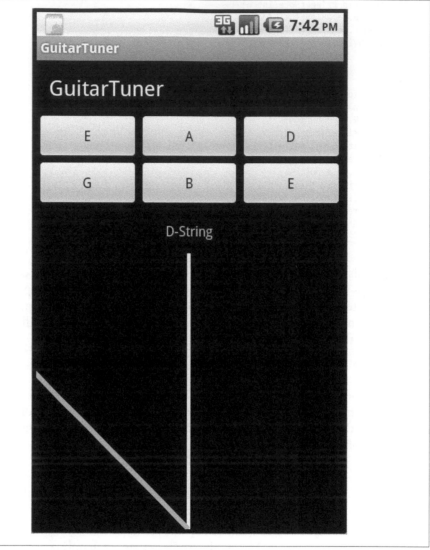

Figure 5-7. The completed guitar tuner app

Building Externals for Android

You can supply your own externals for use with Android if you wish. The details of native Android development are beyond the scope of this book, and so we'll just briefly outline the steps it takes to build and package externals for Android.

If an external is part of Pd Extended, then its build system already includes support for Android and you merely have to invoke make with the right parameters. You can find details at *http://puredata.info/docs/developer/BuildingPdForAndroid*.

If you need to implement build support for Android, you can mimic the approach of the build system of libpd. The file *libpd/Android.mk* shows how to compile externals (e.g., `fiddle~`) for Android, and the file *PdCore/Makefile* shows how to prepare them for deployment.

If you're aiming for compatibility with a wide range of devices, you should consider compiling binaries for both ARMv6 and ARMv7 processors; the make files of PdCore will show you how.

When you have built your externals, you can package them as zip files (say, *ext.zip* for ARMv6 and *ext_v7a.zip* for ARMv7), and copy them to the *res/raw* folder of your project. Now you only need to unpack them, e.g., in the `onCreate` method of your app, and add their location to the search path of Pd. The Android branch of libpd includes a class, *Properties.java*, that will detect the processor architecture for you:

```
File dir = getFilesDir();
try {
    IoUtils.extractZipResource(getResources().openRawResource(
        Properties.hasArmeabiV7a ? R.raw.ext_v7a : R.raw.ext), dir, false);
} catch (IOException e) {
    Log.e(PD_SERVICE, e.toString());
}
PdBase.addToSearchPath(dir.getAbsolutePath());
```

 Android will not let you load externals from the SD card because the SD card is mounted without execution privileges. That's a good thing, because loading executable code from external storage is highly insecure. If you try it anyway, the attempt will fail with a most unhelpful error message. If you've thought through the security issues and you still want to load an external from the SD card, you need to copy it to internal memory first.

CHAPTER 6

Pd for iOS

Core Audio and its audio unit plugin architecture are an excellent platform for making musical apps. Nonetheless, audio units are laborious to configure, and surprising and occasionally subtle problems do come up. As is its wont, however, libpd will protect app developers from platform-specific quirks as much as possible. For instance, early models of the iPod Touch exhibit subtle differences in their floating point representations of buffer durations, causing glitches due to mismatched buffers. Once we had diagnosed the problem, a workaround was easy to find, and users of recent versions of libpd won't even notice this problem anymore.

Different devices come with different audio capabilities. For example, on iPhones you can expect to receive audio input from the microphone, while iPods don't even have microphones. That much is obvious, but there are also less obvious configuration issues, such as audio session categories that are available on some devices but not on others.

When developing a new app, you should test it on a range of different iOS devices, and you should be prepared to try various audio configurations in case the one you want is unavailable or unusable. The libpd community maintains a wiki page that keeps track of devices and audio configurations. If you are using a combination that's not on the list, please consider documenting your experiences on this page, regardless of whether your combination works or not.

As far as sophisticated audio work is concerned, the simulator is of little help. It frequently produces glitchy audio, and even though we make an effort to identify audio configurations that work with the simulator, this is only a stopgap measure that tends to fail as soon as the next update of the simulator comes out. You may be lucky and find a configuration that works, but in general you should consider the iOS simulator a moving target.

Setting Up the Development Environment

We will limit our discussion of iOS development to the latest version of Apple's integrated development environment, Xcode 4.2. Even though Xcode 4.2 has built-in support for Git, it will not suffice for our purposes because of its limited support for submodules. In order to download a copy of the iOS branch of libpd, open a terminal (*Applications/Utilities/Terminal.app*), change into the directory where you want to keep your installation of libpd, and enter the following commands:

```
$ git clone git://github.com/libpd/pd-for-ios.git
$ cd pd-for-ios
$ git submodule init
$ git submodule update
```

This will install libpd and its audio glue for iOS as well as utilities and a few sample apps. It is good practice to keep your copy of libpd up to date. In order to do that, you should regularly issue the following commands in your *pd-for-ios* directory:

```
$ git pull
$ git submodule update
```

You should try the sample apps now in order to make sure that your installation is working. In order to test a sample project, just open its *.xcodeproj* file.

When you open a project for the first time, select the menu item "Product → Manage Schemes...". You should see two schemes, one for the current project and one for libpd, labeled `libpd-ios` (Figure 6-1). Xcode sometimes gets confused when autocreating schemes, though, and if you've been using libpd since before the move to GitHub, then you may end up with a spurious second scheme for libpd, labeled `libpd`, which you can safely delete.

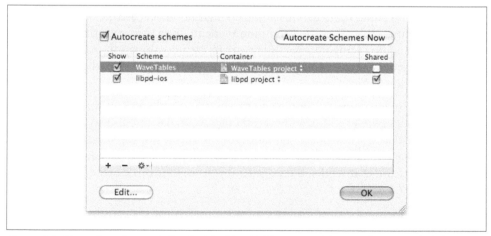

Figure 6-1. Managing schemes in Xcode 4.2. WaveTables is one of the sample apps included with the libpd distribution.

If you try to run a sample app and nothing happens, check the active scheme in the upper righthand corner of Xcode (Figure 6-2). It should display the name of the current project, *not* libpd-ios. If it doesn't, open the Scheme pop-up menu and select the main scheme of the project.

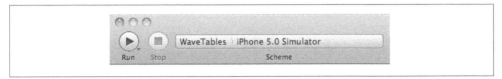

Figure 6-2. Checking the active scheme

None of the sample projects are terribly exciting, but that's intentional. They are supposed to illustrate key points about libpd development for iOS; any visual or musical dazzle would distract from their main purpose.

Creating a Musical App: Part I

As in Chapter 5, we'll create a guitar tuner app. Our first version will be just a digital tuning fork, emitting reference tones on demand. Think of it as *Hello World!* for libpd.

In order to use libpd in an app, you need to import the libpd Xcode project into your project and wire it up so that the editor, compiler, and linker can find the necessary resources. Xcode 4.2 makes this initial setup rather hard, and it is frequently easier to copy a sample project and modify it for your purposes. Nevertheless, we'll ignore the sample projects for now and build our guitar tuner app from scratch.

In Xcode, select File → New → New Project and ask the new project wizard to create the scaffolding of a Single View Application (Figure 6-3).

Now Xcode presents a number of options for our app (Figure 6-4). We need to choose a name for our app, e.g., **GuitarTuner**, a company identifier, and a prefix, e.g., **GT**, that the new project wizard will prepend to the classes that it generates. In order to streamline the exposition, we'll limit ourselves to iPhone apps for now, but everything we discuss in this chapter applies to iPad apps as well. We won't need storyboards in our single-view app, but we will use automatic reference counting (ARC) because that's what Apple recommends for new development.

Importing libpd

Click on the menu item "File → Add Files to "GuitarTuner"…" and add the file *libpd.xcodeproj*. Now libpd should show up as a subproject of your project (Figure 6-5).

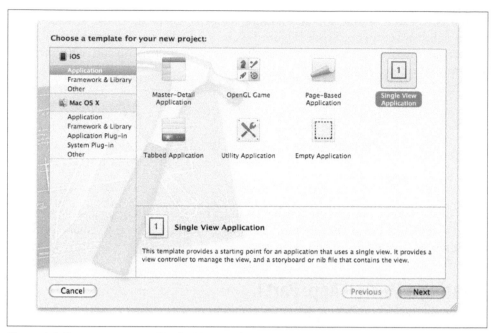

Figure 6-3. Project creation in Xcode 4.2

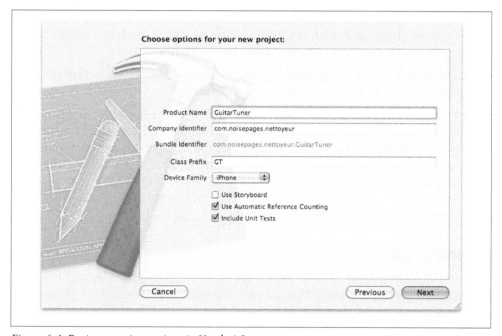

Figure 6-4. Project creation options in Xcode 4.2

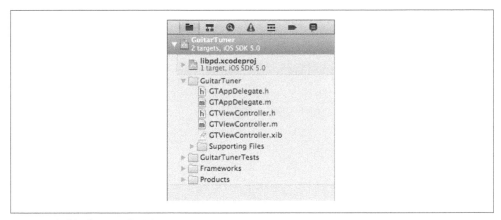

Figure 6-5. libpd in Xcode 4.2

Click on `GuitarTuner` in the Project Navigator to get to the main project settings and check that `GuitarTuner` is selected under Targets. The settings will open on the Summary tab (Figure 6-6). Take this opportunity to deselect all screen orientations except portrait. Later, when you have a sense of how the audio components interact with the rest of the app, you may want to revisit the question of which screen orientations to support. For now, orientation changes are just one more potential point of failure and so we'll disallow them, the faster to get our app off the ground.

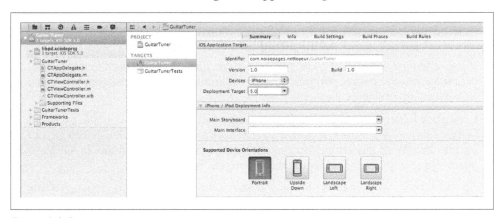

Figure 6-6. Project settings

Now select the Build Settings tab. In the second bar from the top, select All and Combined, then enter the search term **user header**. Find the row labeled "User Header Search Paths" and double-click in the right column, the one corresponding to your current target. A little dialog window will pop up. Now click on +, then select the box labeled `recursive`, and finally enter the path to your libpd installation (Figure 6-7). If you've placed both your new project and your copy of Pd for iOS in your *Documents* folder, then the path *$(SRCROOT)/../../pd-for-ios/libpd* should work.

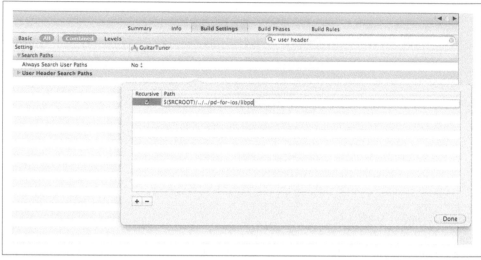

Figure 6-7. Header path settings

 While the entire setup is tedious, the header search path is the only part that's error-prone. If you encounter build problems later on, you should first check whether your search path is correct.

Configuring for Portability

If you're going to share your code with other developers, then you need to take special care to make your project portable. The best solution is probably the approach of Pd for iOS, using git submodules.

Create one folder that will hold both your project folder and a copy of libpd, packaged as a git submodule (just libpd, cloned directly from *git://github.com/libpd/libpd.git*, not Pd for iOS). With this setup, you can use a simple relative path, *$(SRCROOT)/../../ libpd*, and your header search path will be portable.

An added benefit of packaging libpd as a git submodule is that it avoids version conflicts down the road. The submodule of your project will specify the version of libpd to use, and users of your code will automatically receive this version when they clone your project. When you choose to upgrade to a new version of libpd, users of your code will receive the same upgrade when they update their local copy.

Select the Build Phases tab, open the Target Dependencies section and click on +, then add `libpd-ios` as a dependency. Finally, open the "Link Binaries With Libraries" section and add *libpd-ios.a*, *AudioToolbox.framework*, and *AVFoundation.framework* (Figure 6-8). Don't worry if Xcode renders the entry for *libpd-ios.a* in red; it's a known bug of Xcode that won't cause any trouble.

Figure 6-8. Configuring build phases

Unfortunately, Xcode does not know that the static library *libpd-ios.a* and the header search path are related. If you keep more than one copy of libpd around, then it is easy to get confused and import a binary from one and header files from another, potentially leading to hard-to-track build failures where the compiler succeeds but the linker fails.

This completes our initial setup of a new project with libpd. Whew! It was a lot of work, but it's done now.

Configuring libpd

Let's add a Pd patch to our app. As in Chapter 5, we use a straightforward modification of our synthesizer patch from Chapter 2 (Figure 6-9). Click on the menu item "File → Add File to "GuitarTuner"..." and select the folder containing your patch. Xcode offers a number of ways of importing folders; make sure to select "Create groups for any added folders" before clicking on Add (Figure 6-10).

Now we set up the components of libpd as discussed in "Launch Sequence" on page 57. First, we need to configure the audio components of libpd, using an instance of the `PdAudioController` class discussed in Chapter 4. The audio controller is a global object, potentially relevant to all parts of the app, and so we have the application delegate manage it and make it available through an accessor method.

The application delegate interface GTAppDelegate.h.

```
#import <UIKit/UIKit.h>

#import "PdAudioController.h"

@class GTViewController;

@interface GTAppDelegate : UIResponder <UIApplicationDelegate>
```

```
@property (strong, nonatomic) UIWindow *window;
@property (strong, nonatomic) GTViewController *viewController;

@property (strong, nonatomic, readonly) PdAudioController *audioController;

@end
```

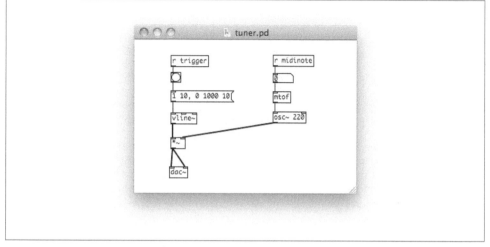

Figure 6-9. Guitar tuner patch (first version)

When designing a musical app with libpd, one of the basic decisions is how to manage the life of the audio thread. In this simple example, we'll take the most straightforward approach and tie the life of the audio thread to the active life of the app. In other words, the audio thread will be active whenever our app is active.

 Tying the lifecycle of the audio thread to the lifecycle of the app is a quick and convenient way to get a new audio project off the ground. I start most new projects that way. If necessary, I revisit the management of the audio thread later, after I've implemented enough of the audio functionality to allow for meaningful testing.

The next code example shows an implementation of this approach. We create and configure the audio controller on launch, and we check the return value in case something goes wrong. In this simple example, we just log a warning and give up if the desired configuration is not available. In real-world code, you will need to implement some graceful way of handling configuration failures, and you may want to try a number of different configurations until you find one that works. In any case, the configuration that we are requesting here, two output channels at CD sample rate with an ambient audio session category, is common and will probably be available.

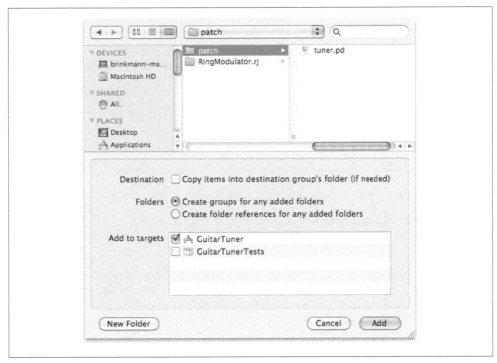

Figure 6-10. Importing the patch into Xcode

The application delegate implementation GTAppDelegate.m.

```
#import "GTAppDelegate.h"

#import "GTViewController.h"

@implementation GTAppDelegate

@synthesize window = _window;
@synthesize viewController = _viewController;
@synthesize audioController = _audioController;

-(BOOL)application:(UIApplication *)application
  didFinishLaunchingWithOptions:(NSDictionary *)launchOptions {
    _audioController = [[PdAudioController alloc] init];
    if ([self.audioController configureAmbientWithSampleRate:44100
            numberChannels:2 mixingEnabled:YES] != PdAudioOK) {
        NSLog(@"failed to initialize audio components");
    }
    self.window = [[UIWindow alloc] initWithFrame:[[UIScreen mainScreen] bounds]];
    self.viewController = [[GTViewController alloc]
                          initWithNibName:@"GTViewController" bundle:nil];
    self.window.rootViewController = self.viewController;
    [self.window makeKeyAndVisible];
    return YES;
}
```

```
// Without ARC, we would need to implement a dealloc method that
// releases _audioController.

-(void)applicationDidBecomeActive:(UIApplication *)application {
    self.audioController.active = YES;
}

-(void)applicationWillResignActive:(UIApplication *)application {
    self.audioController.active = NO;
}

- (void)applicationDidEnterBackground:(UIApplication *)application { }

- (void)applicationWillEnterForeground:(UIApplication *)application { }

- (void)applicationWillTerminate:(UIApplication *)application { }
@end
```

The Objective-C components of libpd provide fine-grained support for managing audio configurations. You can choose to allow ambient audio as well as mixing, and the controller class will automatically choose the appropriate audio session category. You can also reconfigure the audio components on the fly.

Moreover, the audio controller class implements the AVAudioSession Delegate protocol. An instance of PdAudiocontroller will register itself as the audio session delegate, and it will automatically suspend playback when a phone call comes in. If this is not the desired behavior, or if you want to implement additional functionality (such as having the audio fade in and out instead of just turning it on and off), then you can simply create a subclass of PdAudioController and override the methods whose behavior you'd like to change.

Now we register a dispatcher object with libpd. While we don't expect to receive any messages from Pd for the time being, the dispatcher may still come in handy because it will log status messages that Pd prints to the console.

We need to decide which part of our app should be responsible for managing the dispatcher. Since the main purpose of dispatcher is to receive messages from Pd, and since those messages will typically affect the user interface, we'll put the view controller in charge of managing the dispatcher.

After registering the receiver, we open our patch, also in the view controller. In order to open a patch, we need to specify the name of the file and the path to the folder that contains it. Because of the way we packaged the patch, we can simply invoke [[NSBundle mainBundle] resourcePath] in order to get the path.

The view controller interface GTViewController.h.

```
#import <UIKit/UIKit.h>

#import "PdDispatcher.h"

@interface GTViewController : UIViewController {
    PdDispatcher *dispatcher;
    void *patch;
}

@end
```

The view controller implementation GTViewController.m.

```
#import "GTViewController.h"

@implementation GTViewController

#pragma mark - View lifecycle

-(void)viewDidLoad {
    [super viewDidLoad];
    dispatcher = [[PdDispatcher alloc] init];
    [PdBase setDelegate:dispatcher];
    patch = [PdBase openFile:@"tuner.pd"
                        path:[[NSBundle mainBundle] resourcePath]];
    if (!patch) {
        NSLog(@"Failed to open patch!");
        // Gracefully handle failure...
    }
}

-(void)viewDidUnload {
    [super viewDidUnload];
    [PdBase closeFile:patch];
    [PdBase setDelegate:nil];
}

// Omitting the remaining view controller methods...
@end
```

The cleanup in the viewDidUnload method is not strictly necessary in this simple app, but it is good practice to remain aware of the resources that we are consuming and to release them as soon as possible. Even with ARC, there are some resources that will not be automatically released, such as Pd patches and the delegate of PdBase.

In principle, we already have a musical app. All the crucial pieces are present and working; if you launch the app, it will load a patch, start an audio thread and render samples. A dispatcher is installed and ready to receive messages from Pd. If you watch the log messages when launching the app, you'll see that the audio components are being configured and started. We just don't hear anything yet because the app doesn't yet trigger any sounds. We'll remedy that next.

Connecting the User Interface

In order to have our patch make sounds, we will add a few buttons to our user interface. Each will trigger a note corresponding to a string on the guitar. The first step is to add the necessary callback functions to our view controller (see the next code example).

The view controller interface (GTViewController.h) with callback methods.

```
#import <UIKit/UIKit.h>

#import "PdDispatcher.h"

@interface GTViewController : UIViewController {
    PdDispatcher *dispatcher;
    void *patch;
}

-(IBAction)playE:(id)sender;
-(IBAction)playA:(id)sender;
-(IBAction)playD:(id)sender;
-(IBAction)playG:(id)sender;
-(IBAction)playB:(id)sender;
-(IBAction)playE2:(id)sender;

@end
```

This is just the standard boilerplate for connecting UI elements to your code. The most interesting part is our implementation of the callback methods (see the code example below). Each callback sends a MIDI note value to the patch (40 for the low E-string, 45 for the A-string, etc.) and triggers a sound.

The view controller implementation (GTViewController.m) with callback methods.

```
#pragma mark - button callbacks

-(void)playNote:(int)n {
    [PdBase sendFloat:n toReceiver:@"midinote"];
    [PdBase sendBangToReceiver:@"trigger"];
}

-(IBAction)playE:(id)sender {
    NSLog(@"Playing E");
    [self playNote:40];
}

-(IBAction)playA:(id)sender {
    NSLog(@"Playing A");
    [self playNote:45];
}

-(IBAction)playD:(id)sender {
    NSLog(@"Playing D");
    [self playNote:50];
```

```
    }

    -(IBAction)playG:(id)sender {
        NSLog(@"Playing G");
        [self playNote:55];
    }

    -(IBAction)playB:(id)sender {
        NSLog(@"Playing B");
        [self playNote:59];
    }

    -(IBAction)playE2:(id)sender {
        NSLog(@"Playing E2");
        [self playNote:64];
    }
```

Finally, we create some buttons in the user interface and connect them to our callback methods. Open *GTViewController.xib* in the Interface Builder and add six buttons to the view, one for each string on the guitar. You can assign appropriate titles in the Attribute Inspector tab on the right. If you select *File's Owner* in the column on the left and open the connections tab on the right, you will see our newly created callback methods. Connect each method to the appropriate button event (Figure 6-11).

In this example, I have chosen to trigger sounds when the user first touches a button. This is slightly unusual; the standard behavior of buttons is to trigger actions on release. Still, I believe that this is the correct choice for musical apps. After all, you will hear a sound the moment you press a key on a piano, not when you release it.

If you launch your app now, you can push the buttons and hear the corresponding sounds. You may need to plug in headphones if your built-in speakers are unable to render low frequencies.

This simple example goes a long way towards building musical apps. Most of the major pieces are already in place. Clearly, our app has lots of room for improvement, but it serves its purpose: It shows the anatomy of a simple libpd-based app with a minimum of code. As an exercise, you may want to try and improve this app. Here are a few topics to think about:

- Sending a float and a bang when playing a sound is somewhat redundant. How can you revise the patch so that a midi note message also acts as a trigger? (Hint: Look up triggers in Pd.)
- The sound is quite boring. Can you replace the osc~ object with another sound that sounds more interesting? (Hint: Look up the phasor~ object for a quick and dirty change, or read up on synthesis techniques and try something more sophisticated.)

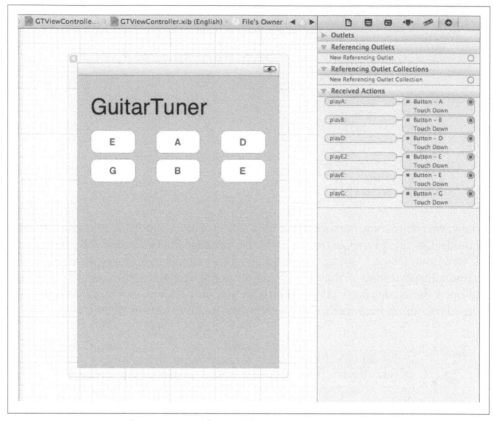

Figure 6-11. Connecting buttons in Interface Builder

Creating a Musical App: Part II

As in Chapter 5, we modify our patch by adding a `fiddle~` object that performs pitch analysis on the microphone input. The patch will send float values to the symbol `pitch` when `fiddle~` detects a stable pitch (Figure 6-12).

Make sure to update the copy of the patch in your Xcode project. Also, since the new version of our patch requires audio input, we need to request input channels when configuring the audio components:

```
-(BOOL)application:(UIApplication *)application
  didFinishLaunchingWithOptions:(NSDictionary *)launchOptions {
    _audioController = [[PdAudioController alloc] init];
    if ([self.audioController configurePlaybackWithSampleRate:44100
            numberChannels:2 inputEnabled:YES mixingEnabled:NO] != PdAudioOK) {
        NSLog(@"failed to initialize audio components");
    }
    self.window = [[UIWindow alloc] initWithFrame:[[UIScreen mainScreen] bounds]];
    self.viewController = [[GTViewController alloc]
                            initWithNibName:@"GTViewController" bundle:nil];
```

```
    self.window.rootViewController = self.viewController;
    [self.window makeKeyAndVisible];
    return YES;
}
```

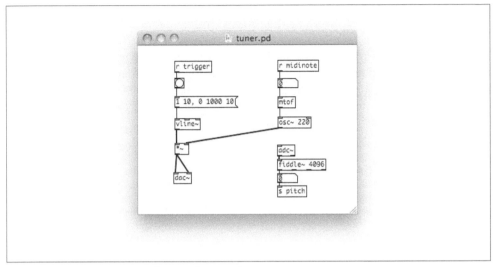

Figure 6-12. Guitar tuner patch (second version)

Receiving Messages from Pd

The patch is now ready to send messages to the app, but the app isn't listening yet. We first have our view controller implement the PdListener protocol (see the section Listener interface in Objective-C on page 50). All methods in the listener protocol are optional, and so we only implement receiveFloat, the method that is relevant to us right now.

Implementing the PdListener protocol.

```
@interface GTViewController : UIViewController<PdListener> {
    PdDispatcher *dispatcher;
    void *patch;
}

-(IBAction)playE:(id)sender;
-(IBAction)playA:(id)sender;
-(IBAction)playD:(id)sender;
-(IBAction)playG:(id)sender;
-(IBAction)playB:(id)sender;
-(IBAction)playE2:(id)sender;

-(void)receiveFloat:(float)value fromSource:(NSString *)source;

@end
```

In this simple example, we just have the view controller class implement the PdListener protocol. As soon as you have more than one send symbol in Pd, however, you will probably want to create separate classes that implement the listener protocol, typically one for each send symbol.

Now we modify the viewDidLoad method so that the view controller registers itself as a listener, and we create a preliminary implementation of receiveFloat that just logs any values that it receives. We will revisit this method later, but for now simple logging is enough to set up and test communications between Pd and our app.

Implementing and Registering a Listener.

```
#pragma mark - View lifecycle

-(void)viewDidLoad {
    [super viewDidLoad];
    dispatcher = [[PdDispatcher alloc] init];
    [dispatcher addListener:self forSource:@"pitch"];
    [PdBase setDelegate:dispatcher];
    patch = [PdBase openFile:@"tuner.pd" path:[[NSBundle mainBundle] resourcePath]];
}

#pragma mark - PdListener callbacks

-(void)receiveFloat:(float)value fromSource:(NSString *)source {
    NSLog(@"received float: %f", value);
}
```

The addListener method of PdDispatcher informs Pd that we want to receive messages sent from the symbol pitch. It also adds our listener to the list of recipients of messages sent from pitch.

This completes the setup of the pub/sub pattern illustrated in Figure 4-2. The dispatcher receives messages from Pd, and it also manages listeners and subscriptions for send symbols. If you whistle or sing into the microphone of your device, however, you won't see any log messages from the listener object. What's wrong?

A quick look at the log messages shows that Pd was unable to create the fiddle~ object. (This illustrates why it's a good idea to always register a dispatcher object, regardless of whether you intend to add listeners for specific send symbols. Without the dispatcher, the log messages would have been lost.)

Using Externals

The problem is that fiddle~ is not a built-in object of Pd but an *external*, i.e., a shared library that Pd will load as needed. This poses two problems for us. By itself, libpd does not provide a shared library for fiddle~, and even if it did, we wouldn't be able to use it here because iOS does not allow dynamic loading of shared libraries.

Fortunately, there is a simple solution. First, we need to add the external to our project, either as source code or as a static library. For the `fiddle~` external, we find the source code in *libpd/pure-data/extra/fiddle~/fiddle~.c* and add it to the group that contains our app delegate and view controller (Figure 6-13).

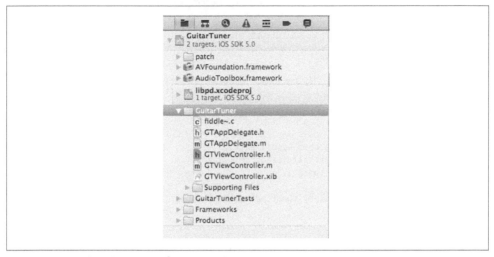

Figure 6-13. Adding the source of an external

Like many other externals, `fiddle~` is designed to work with both Pd and Max/MSP, and we need to set a compiler flag that will activate the Pd-specific parts and hide the parts that are for Max/MSP only. To this end, we go back to the build settings of our project (where we previously set the header search path), enter the search term **other c flags**, and add the flag **-DPD** (Figure 6-14).

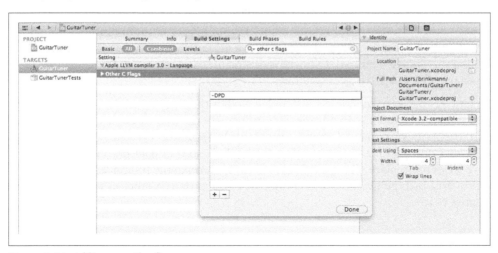

Figure 6-14. Adding compiler flags

Each external has a setup function that registers the external with Pd. As a matter of fact, the only difference between externals and built-in objects is that the setup methods of built-in objects are called by the initialization function of Pd, while externals are registered as needed. In order to register `fiddle~`, we need to call `fiddle_tilde_setup()` after libpd is initialized but before opening the patch. The initialization of libpd happens implicitly when `PdBase` is first accessed, and so we can simply invoke `fiddle_tilde_setup` in `viewDidLoad`, after registering the dispatcher.

```
#pragma mark - View lifecycle

void fiddle_tilde_setup();  // Optional function declaration to address compiler
warnings.

-(void)viewDidLoad {
    [super viewDidLoad];
    dispatcher = [[PdDispatcher alloc] init];
    [dispatcher addListener:self forSource:@"pitch"];
    [PdBase setDelegate:dispatcher];
    fiddle_tilde_setup();
    patch = [PdBase openFile:@"tuner.pd" path:[[NSBundle mainBundle]
resourcePath]];
}
```

The file *fiddle.c* was only meant to be compiled into a dynamically loaded library, and so it does not come with a header file that declares the setup function. We work around this by providing our own declaration of `fiddle_tilde_setup`.

 If you want to distribute your app through Apple's App Store, you need to pay special attention to the licensing of externals. Many externals are covered by the GNU General Public License, which is *not* compatible with App Store rules. This used to be the case for the popular **expr** family of externals, but they have recently been released under a different license, the GNU *Lesser* General Public License.

If you launch the app now, you will first see a log entry indicating that Pd successfully loaded the `fiddle~` external, followed by a stream of log entries showing the float messages that the `fiddle~` object generates.

So far, our message callback is just a placeholder that logs events as it receives them. The last step is to hook up our message callback to the user interface. To this end, we add the line `@property (strong, nonatomic) IBOutlet UILabel *pitchLabel;` to *GTViewController.h* and `@synthesize pitchLabel;` to *GTViewController.m*. With the new property in place, we open *GTViewController.xib* in the Interface Builder, include a property of type `UILabel`, and connect the property to a label in Interface Builder (Figure 6-15).

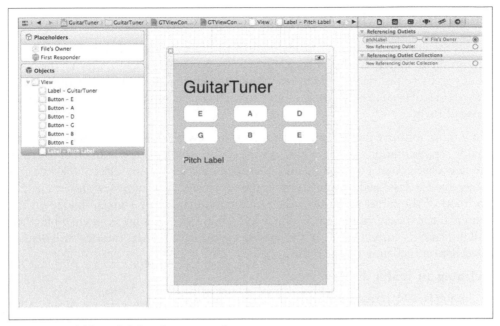

Figure 6-15. Adding a label to the user interface

Next, we modify our listener callback so that it updates the pitch label when it receives a new float message:

```
#pragma mark - PdListener callbacks

-(void)receiveFloat:(float)value {
    pitchLabel.text = [NSString stringWithFormat:@"Pitch: %f", value, nil];
}
```

 Even though the pitch messages originate on the audio thread, the PdBase class invokes message callbacks on the main thread, and so our callback method can manipulate the user interface directly, without having to pay attention to concurrency issues.

If you launch the app now, you'll see a steady stream of pitch values in the UI label. Most of the time the displayed values will be quite random as fiddle~ finds odd pitches in ambient noise. If you hum or whistle into the microphone, however, you will see that the pitch values stabilize. The communication between Pd and our app is working, in both directions!

Improving the User Interface

While the current version is already enough to illustrate the way libpd handles the communication between Pd and our app, it is not yet terribly useful. After all, the pitch values go by so fast that is hard to read them, and even if we could follow the output, we would still need to know the meaning of MIDI note values by heart in order to make sense of them.

For a more intuitive display, we create a custom view class, `PitchView`, that shows an analog representation of pitch values (see the code examples below). (In order to create the new class, open a context menu for the *GuitarTuner* group, select "New File... → Objective-C Class" and choose `UIView` as the superclass.) The new view shows a neighborhood of the target pitch, with the target pitch marked by a green line down the center. If the measured pitch is within a few semitones of the target pitch, a blue line will indicate its current value. If it is outside the displayed range, the view will display a red bar on the left or on the right.

Defining an analog display.

```
@interface PitchView : UIView { }

@property(nonatomic) float centerPitch;
@property(nonatomic) float currentPitch;

@end
```

Implementing an analog display.

```
#import <math.h>
#import "PitchView.h"

@implementation PitchView

@synthesize centerPitch = _centerPitch;
@synthesize currentPitch = _currentPitch;

-(id)initWithFrame:(CGRect)frame {
    self = [super initWithFrame:frame];
    if (self) {
        // Initialization code
    }
    return self;
}

-(void)setCenterPitch:(float)centerPitch {
    _centerPitch = centerPitch;
    [self setNeedsDisplay];
}

-(void)setCurrentPitch:(float)currentPitch {
    _currentPitch = currentPitch;
    [self setNeedsDisplay];
}
```

```
-(void)drawRect:(CGRect)rect {
    float halfWidth = self.frame.size.width / 2;
    float height = self.frame.size.height;

    CGContextRef context = UIGraphicsGetCurrentContext();
    CGContextSetLineWidth(context, 6.0);
    CGContextSetStrokeColorWithColor(context, [UIColor greenColor].CGColor);
    CGContextMoveToPoint(context, halfWidth, 0);
    CGContextAddLineToPoint(context, halfWidth, height);
    CGContextStrokePath(context);

    float dx = (self.currentPitch - self.centerPitch) / 2;
    if (-1 < dx && dx < 1) {
        CGContextSetLineWidth(context, 2.0);
        CGContextSetStrokeColorWithColor(context, [UIColor blueColor].CGColor);
    } else {
        CGContextSetLineWidth(context, 8.0);
        CGContextSetStrokeColorWithColor(context, [UIColor redColor].CGColor);
        dx = (dx < 0) ? -1 : 1;
    }
    float phi = dx * M_PI_4;
    CGContextMoveToPoint(context, halfWidth, height);
    CGContextAddLineToPoint(context, halfWidth + sin(phi) * height * 0.9,
                                     height - cos(phi) * height * 0.9);
    CGContextStrokePath(context);
}

// Omitting some boilerplate...
@end
```

The PitchView class has two properties, the target pitch and the current pitch, and it offers a pair of accessors for updating them. Graphics programming is beyond the scope of this book, and so we won't discuss the implementation of the PitchView class in detail. It is fairly straightforward, though, and a casual reading of the drawRect: method will give you a good idea of how it works.

We hook up the new view in the usual way—import *PitchView.h* and add the line @property (strong, nonatomic) IBOutlet PitchView *pitchView; to *GTViewController.h*, then synthesize the property in *GTViewController.m*. In the Interface Builder, add a new UIView object to the user interface, then go the Identity Inspector tab on the right and choose PitchView under Custom Class (Figure 6-16). Now you can open the Connections Inspector on the right and connect your new PitchView object to the pitch View property of the view controller.

Since we now have a visual representation of the measured pitch, we now longer have to display a textual representation. This frees up the pitch label for another use. We'll simply have it display the current center pitch of our custom view. In order to give the user a visual clue that the label says something about the center pitch, we change its text alignment property in the Attributes Inspector to center.

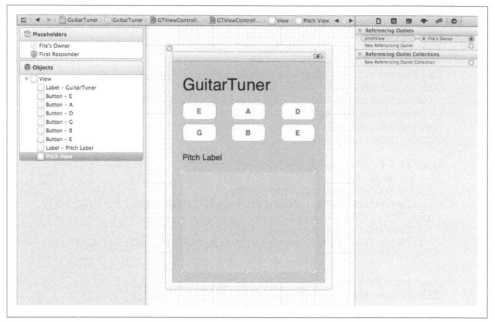

Figure 6-16. Adding a custom view

Finally, we adjust the view controller class so that it properly initializes and updates the new pitch view. When the user triggers a reference tone for a string, we'll also set the center pitch to this string and update the pitch label accordingly.

The last revision of GTViewController.m.

```
#pragma mark - View lifecycle

-(void)viewDidLoad {
    [super viewDidLoad];
    pitchView.centerPitch = 45;
    pitchLabel.text = @"A-String";
    dispatcher = [[PdDispatcher alloc] init];
    [dispatcher addListener:self forSource:@"pitch"];
    [PdBase setDelegate:dispatcher];
    fiddle_tilde_setup();
    patch = [PdBase openFile:@"tuner.pd" path:[[NSBundle mainBundle] resourcePath]];
}

#pragma mark - button callbacks

-(void)playNote:(int)n {
    pitchView.centerPitch = n;
    [PdBase sendFloat:n toReceiver:@"midinote"];
    [PdBase sendBangToReceiver:@"trigger"];
}
```

```
-(IBAction)playE:(id)sender {
    pitchLabel.text = @"E-string (low)";
    [self playNote:40];
}

-(IBAction)playA:(id)sender {
    pitchLabel.text = @"A-string";
    [self playNote:45];
}

// And so on...

#pragma mark - PdListener callbacks

-(void)receiveFloat:(float)value fromSource:(NSString *)source {
    pitchView.currentPitch = value;
}
```

That's it! We now have a complete and usable guitar tuner app (Figure 6-17).

This simple example has introduced us to all major aspects of developing iOS apps with libpd. It also shows how I go about developing a libpd-based app. None of the steps is there for didactic purposes only. If I had written this app by myself, without the intention of explaining how to create a musical app, I still would have proceeded in the exact same way.

The general strategy is to get *something* to work as quickly as possible, and then to arrive at the desired functionality through a sequence of small adjustments, trying each revision as I go along. Refining a crude but working app is faster and easier than trying to build a sophisticated app from scratch.

There's still lots of room for improvement. Here are a few ideas:

- While the app is already usable, it still looks quite plain. How would you design a better user interface?
- The fiddle~ object always generates pitch values, even when you aren't playing any notes on your guitar. Modify the patch so that it will only output pitch values for input signals whose volume exceeds a certain threshold. (Hint: In addition to objects that we've already seen, you may want to use threshold~ and spigot.)
- The pitch values seem a bit jittery when you first pluck a string on your guitar. How would you smoothen the pitch values? You might apply signal processing techniques in Pd, or you might have your app interpolate between successive values, possibly using the built-in animation capabilities of iOS. What are the trade-offs?

Figure 6-17. The finished app

CHAPTER 7

Outlook

We have reached the end of our introduction to making musical apps with libpd. It's been a short book, but then again, libpd is a small library. You now have all the technical knowledge you'll need if you want to make musical apps for Android and iOS. You have learned how to patch for libpd, how to code with libpd, and how to define the interface between audio and application code. Of course, many challenges remain — coming up with a good idea, creating a great patch, designing a compelling user interface, tweaking parameters until they are just right, and so on. All this takes work and patience and experience, but the potential payoff is immense. I truly believe that artists and engineers have barely begun to explore the musical possibilities of ubiquitous mobile devices with numerous sensors and powerful CPUs.

We have focused on the basic software development kits for Android and iOS, but most of the ideas and techniques we discussed apply to other platforms as well. At the time of writing, libpd already includes support for C++ , Processing, openFrameworks, and Python. Processing has been ported to Android, and openFrameworks to iOS, and so they offer yet another way of creating musical apps with libpd. One team has already built an app with libpd and Adobe AIR; support for PhoneGap might be in the offing. Several people have expressed interest in support for .NET or Mono, and it is only a matter of time until somebody creates C# bindings for libpd.

Unfortunately, there is one significant constraint that limits the utility of libpd. The current version of Pd is a singleton; it is not possible to create multiple instances of Pd, or to add audio channels on the fly. This isn't much of a concern when Pd is running as originally intended (as a stand-alone desktop application), but it rules out an entire class of use cases that libpd would otherwise be perfect for. For instance, you will come up against this limitation if you want to build an effects processor that doesn't directly connect to the audio channels of the hardware but participates in a plugin architecture where an ever-changing collection of audio components are wired together.

The good news is that this problem won't affect most musical apps because their architecture will be much like that of Pd on the desktop, except that the apps assume the role of the graphical user interface. They only need one audio engine, and their audio channels connect directly to the input and output channels of the hardware, so that the required number of channels will be known at initialization time.

Moreover, Miller Puckette and the other core contributors of Pd are aware of the problem, and they are planning to correct this. When a revised version of Pd removes the limitation to a single instance, a new version of libpd will follow suit, and then even more possibilities will open up.

Since the first Pd patch went beep on an old Motorola Droid on Bastille Day 2010, libpd has grown from a single developer's hobby to a platform with a solid group of core contributors, hundreds of developers, and millions of downloads. A solution that arose out of necessity has turned out to be applicable almost everywhere. It's been a humbling experience to see the outpouring of enthusiasm and creativity that followed the release of libpd, and I am grateful to everybody who helped make libpd a success, whether through active development, creative use, or constructive feedback. I invite you, dear reader, to join us and make mind-blowing musical apps.

About the Author

Peter Brinkmann is the principal developer behind libpd. He has a PhD in mathematics and has published in pure mathematics, virtual reality, and computer music. He has contributed to several open source projects, was a college professor, and is now a software engineer at Google.

Get even more for your money.

Join the O'Reilly Community, and register the O'Reilly books you own. It's free, and you'll get:

- $4.99 ebook upgrade offer
- 40% upgrade offer on O'Reilly print books
- Membership discounts on books and events
- Free lifetime updates to ebooks and videos
- Multiple ebook formats, DRM FREE
- Participation in the O'Reilly community
- Newsletters
- Account management
- 100% Satisfaction Guarantee

Signing up is easy:

1. **Go to: oreilly.com/go/register**
2. **Create an O'Reilly login.**
3. **Provide your address.**
4. **Register your books.**

Note: English-language books only

To order books online:
oreilly.com/store

For questions about products or an order:
orders@oreilly.com

To sign up to get topic-specific email announcements and/or news about upcoming books, conferences, special offers, and new technologies:
elists@oreilly.com

For technical questions about book content:
booktech@oreilly.com

To submit new book proposals to our editors:
proposals@oreilly.com

O'Reilly books are available in multiple DRM-free ebook formats. For more information:
oreilly.com/ebooks

Spreading the knowledge of innovators   oreilly.com

©2010 O'Reilly Media, Inc. O'Reilly logo is a registered trademark of O'Reilly Media, Inc. 00000

The information you need, when and where you need it.

With Safari Books Online, you can:

Access the contents of thousands of technology and business books

- Quickly search over 7000 books and certification guides
- Download whole books or chapters in PDF format, at no extra cost, to print or read on the go
- Copy and paste code
- Save up to 35% on O'Reilly print books
- **New!** Access mobile-friendly books directly from cell phones and mobile devices

Stay up-to-date on emerging topics before the books are published

- Get on-demand access to evolving manuscripts.
- Interact directly with authors of upcoming books

Explore thousands of hours of video on technology and design topics

- Learn from expert video tutorials
- Watch and replay recorded conference sessions